R.B. Hill has extensive experience and expertise in various fields, particularly in social care. With over 20 years of experience, including 11 years specifically focused on working as a social worker with older adults in diverse teams. He has accumulated a wealth of knowledge and understanding. His versatility is evident in his roles as an independent social worker and best interest assessor and his involvement in supporting students and social work consultancy. His commitment to continuous growth and expanding his skill set is commendable. His decision to become a hearing aid dispenser in audiology further exemplifies his dedication to providing comprehensive support to those in need.

By diversifying his expertise, R.B. Hill ensures that he can address a wider range of challenges faced by individuals and offer them the best possible care. What truly sets this author apart is his genuine passion for helping and supporting others, which stems from his own personal journey of overcoming obstacles in life. Having faced and conquered challenges himself, he possesses a deep empathy and understanding for those he works with.

R.B. Hill draws upon his own experiences to forge meaningful connections with individuals, enabling him to guide them through their own challenges and empower them to realise their full potential. He has a sharp, perceptive mind and wealth of experience make him an irreplaceable asset in his profession. He is a master in his field, with a deep understanding of its complexities and an unwavering drive for perfection. This truly sets him apart is his multifaceted background and his genuine empathy for others. These qualities combine to make him a compassionate and highly effective advocate for those he serves. His devotion to helping others and his exceptional skills make him a true standout in his industry.

Embarking on this literary adventure is both exhilarating and nerve-racking. To all the readers who have chosen to join me, thank you for giving me a reason to share my story. Your interest and support mean the world to me.

As I reflect on my life, I am reminded of all the incredible individuals who have shaped me. My family, friends, mentors, and even strangers have all played a significant role in my growth and success. Each of you has left an indelible mark on my heart, and I am forever grateful for your presence in my life.

To my mother,
You were a beacon of strength and courage, never faltering, even in the toughest times. You stood tall and faced challenges without ever showing how low you may have felt inside.

You always made the best out of what you had and never gave up on believing in your dreams. I hope that this book, in a symbolic way, captures the essence of those dreams and what it means to fight until the very end.

To my family, thank you for always being there for me with unwavering love and support. You have encouraged me to push forward and have been there to celebrate every achievement with me.

To my friends, thank you for being a constant source of joy and inspiration. Your friendship has helped me navigate through difficult times and has made the good times even better.

To my mentors, thank you for sharing your wisdom and guidance with me. Your advice has helped shape not only my career but also my character.

And to all the strangers whose paths have crossed mine, thank you for your kind words or gestures that may seem small but have made a big impact on me. Your kindness reminds me of the beauty of humanity.

I am blessed to have each and every one of you in my life, and I am grateful for everything you have done for me. Thank you for being a part of this journey with me.

R.B. Hill

NOTICE ME

AUSTIN MACAULEY PUBLISHERS™

LONDON • CAMBRIDGE • NEW YORK • SHARJAH

A CIP catalogue record for this title is available from the British Library.

ISBN 9781035869800 (Paperback)
ISBN 9781035869817 (ePub e-book)

www.austinmacauley.com

First Published 2024
Austin Macauley Publishers Ltd®
1 Canada Square
Canary Wharf
London
E14 5AA

I would like to express my deepest gratitude to all those who have contributed to the creation and completion of this book, knowingly or unknowingly. Without their support, guidance, and inspiration, this endeavour would not have been possible.

I want to express my gratitude to my beloved wife, our two children and our very first chest freezer. This was purchased with my very first payslip whilst working for the local authority back in 1994 and is still working.

When I started on my employment journey, and in particular, the social work degree in 2009, I was completely overwhelmed with the tools and resources at my disposal. I had never studied at this level before.

At the start of the course, I kept writing and rewriting my first-ever assignment introduction. I was feeling stuck and unsure of the best approach. But you were there by my side, offering valuable advice and support to start me off.

Your constant belief in me and patience stayed with me, regardless of my background and starting point in life. Even back then, my childhood and the journey I had taken so far was a conversation of many possibilities.

We all carry our own baggage, unique backgrounds, hang-ups, and experiences, but you saw past all of that without judgement, no matter where my story began or indeed will end. I will always be eternally grateful. Thank you for standing by me, even during the toughest moments.

Antonio Specchia (Giulio), I want to express my sincere gratitude for your unwavering support and patience throughout the hearing aid dispenser course, in particular the practical hearing assessment.

Your guidance and encouragement undoubtedly prevented me from losing my cool and helped me successfully complete the course. You are a remarkable teacher and a true asset to your profession.

The course not only taught me valuable skills but also allowed me to learn more about myself, with your words serving as a reminder that it's okay to ask for help when needed.

Stephen Campbell, throughout my time with you on the course, I faced countless moments of self-doubt and uncertainty. But your unwavering support and belief in me helped me to trust in my own abilities.

To me, the key to being a successful teacher is effective communication, empathy, and gently pushing students to reach their full potential. And you definitely pushed me to do just that, for which I am grateful.

Akilah Mosely, I will never forget the interview where you saw potential in me to pursue a degree in social work. It was a pivotal moment in my life, and I am grateful and honoured to have been chosen for this incredible journey that has brought me so much personal and educational growth.

This opportunity has taken me to new places and given me opportunities beyond my wildest dreams. The fact that you noticed me was all that I needed.

Patricia Fernando, who would have thought that the next step of my journey would begin with a call from your husband, AJ, inviting me to join Homecare Comforts. Being that I was the fifth person to be interviewed, it is almost as if the tapestry of life had been woven to a certain path and we didn't even know it.

This has been an incredible privilege, and I am grateful for the belief and support you and AJ have given me. The opportunities I have been given far surpass my initial expectations when I first joined. Even though AJ departed from us in tragic circumstances, we continue to progress and excel in everything we do.

I know AJ would be proud of both our personal and professional growth and our future endeavours together are going to be a success story of what we started as three of us. After AJ's sudden departure, you still carried on believing in me and gave me the endless opportunities to go forward and when I needed help, you were always there to give me the support that I needed as a big sister I never had.

So, for that, I owe gratitude and carry it close to my heart for rest of my life. Since coming on board, you, and AJ always showed an interest in hearing about my life's journey and my experiences. It did not feel like I was ever an employee, but part of something special with endless possibilities to explore.

I would always provide snippets through conversation about my life's journey of where I started. I guess this was because AJ's journey was very similar to mine. It was amazing to learn that we grew up in the same place, we went to the same school and we faced difficulties and obstacles along the way.

It was suggested by you that I should write my story because other people need to hear it. I then got to work and over a period of two years of finding the time to write paragraphs, it then became a book.

It has taken some time, but I eventually got there in the end. I welcome the next chapter of the journey of Homecare Comforts and what it will bring.

Janet Holness, you were undeniably a fantastic supervisor and a good friend to me. You have instilled in me what it means to be a good practitioner and a person. I will always carry that with me everywhere I go.

Barry Purdell, our story has a clear beginning, middle, and end. In 2009, during my second placement for social work training, we formed an unexpected bond that transcended into an unforgettable friendship. Your presence in my life has been nothing short of inspiring. Your sense of humour, endless jokes, and unwavering positivity are contagious, often leaving me feeling invigorated and 'concratic'.

Katrena Lawford, what can I say about you? From the moment I met you at the grand Lewisham Town Hall, with its grand marble columns and ornate chandeliers, our lives have been a whirlwind. We landed that coveted job together, and our paths have been intertwined ever since. It's almost as if fate brought us together.

I truly believe that there are certain people we meet in life who are meant to be by our side, and you are one of them. Together, we've experienced the highest highs and lowest lows, facing life's challenges head-on and emerging stronger than ever. Your unwavering strength and goodness make you a true force of nature in this world.

Sharon Byford, even though your social work training was cut short, you are a tribute to the social work profession. Your compassion and understanding make you an invaluable asset, and you have always made yourself available in one way or another—something that cannot be quantified.

Ike Igwegbe, you spring boarded this whole journey by writing a recommendation that I be put forward for the social work degree. You could say that you noticed me first, in the sense of belief that I can do it, and for that, I will forever be grateful.

From day one, Sharon Hamilton, you have been there for us, providing valuable guidance and unwavering encouragement and making sure my wife and I were doing okay. Your kindness, empathy and genuine self will always hold a special place in my heart.

JJ has evolved into an amazing, compassionate person with a heart of pure gold. We are so grateful to have you and JJ in our lives; your impact on us is immeasurable.

To everyone else whom I have not mentioned, I want to take a moment to express my gratitude and appreciation for each and every one of you. There are so many people who have played a role in shaping me into the person I am today and have contributed to my journey in some way.

To my colleagues and teammates throughout the years, thank you for being part of my support system and for being there through the ups and downs. Your camaraderie, teamwork, and dedication have made work more enjoyable and fulfilling.

To my mentors, thank you for guiding me and offering your wisdom and advice. Your experience has been invaluable to me, and I will always be grateful for the lessons I have learnt from you.

To my friends outside of social work, thank you for keeping me grounded and reminding me that there is life outside of work. Your love, support, and laughter have been a constant source of joy in my life.

To all the clients I have had the privilege of working with, thank you for trusting me with your stories and allowing me to be a part of your journey. It has been an honour to walk alongside you as we navigated through challenges together.

A special thanks goes to the team at Austin Macauley Publishing for their expertise, professionalism, and dedication in bringing this book to life. Your tireless efforts and commitment to excellence are deeply appreciated.

I wish to express my appreciation to the reviewers and editors have who meticulously reviewed and provided valuable feedback on the manuscript. Your keen eye for detail and constructive criticism have undoubtedly enhanced the quality of this work.

Lastly, I want to thank the readers who will embark on this literary journey. It is for you that this book has been written, and I hope it brings you knowledge, joy, and inspiration.

In conclusion, I extend my heartfelt appreciation to each and every individual who has played a role in the creation of this book, who may not even know it. Your support, encouragement, and contributions have shaped it into what it is today. Thank you for being a part of this incredible journey.

Table of Contents

Throughout my upbringing, I faced numerous obstacles and roadblocks that could have crushed my spirit. But I refused to let them defeat me. Instead, I adjusted and changed my path to emerge victorious in the midst of chaos.

When I look back on those experiences, it serves as a poignant reminder of our inner strength and capacity to conquer any hardship, rebuild ourselves, and forge our own path towards success.

Endorsements

"As soon as I dived into the world crafted by this talented author, I realised that I had stumbled upon something truly unique."

Ray, you are the ray of true sunshine that never dies as the real sun which keeps going and shining on everyone's life when they are in need with no discrimination.

Life is a challenge full of obstacles, but you took the challenges and obstacles on your own despite the fact that being diagnosed as dyslexic, autistic, bullied and ignored with so-called institutes at such a young age and you turned the life around to your own success and still keep going for new endeavours.

This is why you are so unique and a great example to all humankind promoting the positivity (evident from these memoirs of 'Notice Me') throughout and helping others who need help or who are vulnerable.

Dr Patricia Fernando, Chief B Medical Scientist

The book tugs at the heart but briskly releases it.

Venessa Dotun-Oladeji

Wow, what a life, hun. I can really see how the person I have known for over 30 years is and why. You have been through so much and accomplished (and still accomplishing) so much.

Sharon Hamilton

Prologue

I believe there is a profound truth about life, which is that our starting circumstances are often beyond our control. The circumstances we are born into, such as our family, social status, or economic background, can play a significant role in shaping our initial opportunities and challenges.

Whilst we cannot change our starting point, we do have the power to determine our response to these circumstances. We can choose to accept them as they are and navigate within the confines they present, or we can take proactive steps to change them. It is this choice that holds the potential for personal growth and transformation.

Striving for success, whatever that may mean to each individual, requires resilience, determination, and a willingness to embrace change. It involves recognising the obstacles that exist and finding creative ways to overcome them. This might involve pursuing education, building skills, seeking mentorship, or leveraging opportunities that arise along the way.

Whilst the path to success may be different for some, it is important to remember that success can take on different forms. It is not solely defined by material wealth or external achievements but also by personal fulfilment, happiness, and making a positive impact in our own lives and the lives of others.

By taking ownership of our circumstances, focusing on our strengths, and being proactive in pursuing our goals, we can strive for a sense of comfort and prosperity that aligns with our individual aspirations.

It is through our choices, actions, and resilience we demonstrate that we have the ability to shape our own destinies and make the most out of the hand we are dealt.

At times, I felt that with the hands I had been dealt, my efforts and presence were not enough to make a difference in the world or to be recognised for who I was. This feeling of insignificance undermined my confidence and led me to doubt my strengths. I am sure that many of us can relate to this sensation of being overlooked, unappreciated and unnoticed.

However, I have come to realise that it is not our place to prove ourselves or to live up to the expectations others place upon us. Instead, we must take ownership of our lives and strive for personal fulfilment through whatever means we deem worthy.

This involves taking an honest look at us, setting realistic goals, and committing to taking actionable steps towards achieving them. Through perseverance, resilience, and hard work, we can learn from our mistakes and build on our successes. We can become better versions of ourselves by focusing on our strengths rather than our weaknesses.

We also need to acknowledge that we are not always going to be accepted or appreciated for who we are or what we do. The opinions of others do not define us or legitimise our worth.

We must continue our journey despite the criticism or approval we receive from other people, as it is only by standing up for ourselves that we can truly find strength in our own uniqueness.

Ultimately, embracing who we are enables us to go beyond societal norms and discover a path suited uniquely to each individual's needs and purpose in life. It is a journey of self-discovery that requires courage but leads towards satisfaction and contentment with oneself—and I believe this is one of the most important steps in creating a meaningful life for oneself.

I never imagined that my life would become a memoir or the mere fact that I would write one. But as I reflect on the path I've travelled, I realise the significance of sharing my story.

This memoir is a testament to the resilience of the human spirit and the power of overcoming adversity. Join me as I take you on a deeply personal journey, from the dysfunction of my early years to the triumphs that awaited me.

Although I am excited about releasing this book, I can't help but feel a sense of anxiety and excitement. This is the beginning of my memoir, a deeply personal account of my life that will soon be released to the world. The thought both exhilarates and worries me.

I have always been a private person, rarely sharing my thoughts and feelings with others. Yet here I am, about to lay bare my deepest emotions and experiences for all to see. It's a scary prospect, but one that I believe is necessary in order for me to fully embrace who I am and where I come from.

However, the thought of releasing this memoir also fills me with worry. I wonder how people will perceive my story.

Will they judge me? Will they understand the choices I've made? Will they even care enough to read it?

My family members are at the forefront of my mind as well. Whilst writing this memoir, I have had to confront some uncomfortable truths about my upbringing and relationships within my family. Will they understand my perspective? Will they be hurt or angry by what I have written?

But despite these worries, there is an underlying excitement within me as well. The idea that someone out there might read my story and find comfort or inspiration in it brings me immense joy. Perhaps someone going through similar experiences will feel less alone, knowing that someone else has gone through it, too.

I also hope that by sharing my story, people will be able to see past their own assumptions and prejudices about individuals who come from dysfunctional backgrounds or struggle with mental health issues. My hope is that they will see the resilience and strength within all of us who have faced adversity.

Throughout this process of writing my memoir, one thing has become clear; respect for myself, as well as for those who have played a role in shaping me, is crucial. Despite any potential consequences or backlash, I truly respect my family members and hope that they will understand the intentions behind my story.

When I wrote the book, I was careful not to disclose any specific person's identity. It was a conscious decision motivated by the desire to protect people's privacy and sidestep any legal issues.

I used initials instead of names so that readers could connect to the story without being side-tracked by real-world information. My intention was to focus purely on the message I wanted to convey and let the experiences and emotions speak for themselves.

This creative approach allowed me to discuss themes, share stories, and delve into my personal experiences without disclosing any identities. It provided more freedom to express myself whilst respecting the privacy of those along for the ride.

Being general in my details also invited readers to identify with the overall messages and emotions rather than getting bogged down in the particulars. On top of that, it was a type of safeguard, protecting those involved from potential judgment or unwanted publicity.

Chapter 1
The Beginning

The year was 1971, and the bustling city of London was alive with anticipation for my arrival; well, I like to think so. In Lewisham Hospital, in the heart of Southeast London, I took my first breath.

My mother often told me the story of how she met my father whilst waiting for a bus in Lewisham. Their chance encounter turned into long conversations, and eventually, they got married.

Despite their young age, my father only twenty and my mother twenty-three, they decided to get married. As fate would have it, I was born on the same day as my older sibling, two years apart but forever tied together by our shared birthdate.

Growing up in an environment marked by chaos, disarray, and violence was a difficult experience at home and whilst in school. The long-term physical, mental and emotional scars are evidence of the hardship endured.

It's an unfortunate reality that no one should have to go through. Just imagine a situation suddenly turning hostile, and you're having to worry about your own safety because, as a young kid, you just want to be reassured, and you have very little means to achieve that.

In my later adult years, my mother told me during a conversation that I was quite an ill child, and I nearly died when I was born. She also mentioned that she thought she would have to christen me because she didn't know if I was going to live or not, so she did.

But eventually, later in life, she told me I was not christened. Her 'stories' were a consistent part of my life, though whether or not I'd been christened was unimportant.

In my younger teenage years, as birthdays approached, my mother would tell me that my birthday card or present was in the post, but I didn't receive anything. Even when I reminded her, she would say either it's 'on the way' or it has got 'lost in the post'.

Although I was anticipating nothing, I still had hope that something would come through the post for me to remember that special day. In hindsight, I understand now why she said it.

I have no malice or ill feelings about it or towards my mother. I guess it was an easy way of making me understand either she couldn't afford to buy me anything or she just didn't get anything. But I wished she was honest with me instead.

I guess conversations with a child can get awkward easily, so I can only assume she avoided it. That's probably why I don't care if I receive anything for my birthday or Christmas. I don't expect anyone to get me anything.

Surprises or fancy gifts aren't necessary. I have always been fine receiving nothing and have never liked attention in that form.

As a young child, I felt invisible at times. Feeling unseen and unheard at home and school, I wanted acknowledgement of my thoughts and feelings. It's a constant internal conflict between wanting to not stand out and needing to be noticed.

Often, conversations flowed around me without room for me to join in. My accomplishments were overshadowed by louder voices and brighter personalities, fading away into the background.

This made me question my value within the family dynamic; did I matter? I desired a deeper connection with those closest to me, wanting to be seen and understood. Yet, instead, I found myself cloaked in invisibility, becoming nothing more than a part of the scenery.

In the end, I held onto hope that one day, in my later years, my family would truly see me, not just as a background figure but as an integral part. Until then, I continue to search for my sense of identity and purpose, embracing the unique light that would eventually burn within me, even if it remains unseen by those closest to me.

I don't blame my mother, but it's hard not to be angry about the things I went through as a child and in my early teens. It brings me sadness because of the circumstances she faced in her own life.

She didn't have many opportunities available to her. So, she could hardly support me or my siblings in finding our own paths forward. Yet, despite all this, she did her best with what she had, and I still feel a deep love for her.

She was doing her best with the life she had been dealt with. She'd often remark that she was the 'odd one out' and was classed as the 'black sheep' of the family compared to her siblings.

They all seemed to lead regular lives; they lived in a stable family environment, worked the typical 9-5 and had a house that they owned.

I can still remember as a young kid walking to the local corner shop on the estate where we lived. My mother had asked me to go to the shop with a written note. I would often unfold the note and read it on the way to the corner shop.

It was a shopping list. My mother would ask for help in providing us with groceries from the list and promised to pay for the items later in the week.

At first, I felt awkward and embarrassed, but over the years, I learnt there is no shame in asking for help when needed. The staff at the shop would always be respectful and understanding towards us. I guess times were different back then.

My father left the home when I was very young; my mother told me later she threw him out because he had cheated on her. This much is true since I can't remember him ever being around at home.

The only memories I have as a young boy were visiting my dad to collect child support with my mother. This would be either at his workplace or a shopping centre. My dad felt unfamiliar and distant to me.

Despite his presence, we never really connected; it was always for a specific purpose, not to build any sort of bond as a father and son.

I don't recall when my dad left; I only know that it was after such time that my mother then got involved with a person named J. I don't remember how she met him, but I think he worked as a builder on the estate where we lived.

I would describe J as a man who was brutal, cruel, and domineering, and especially fond of guzzling alcohol. Back then, I was merely a kid who felt powerless to do anything about anyone who entered the house.

It is very difficult, I would say, to grow up without a father figure to look up to. There were my mother's partners throughout my teenage life, but it wasn't the same thing. I felt like growing up in a household where dysfunction and instability weren't the norm.

I longed for stability and guidance that seemed out of reach. Sadly, my mother's choices of partners turned out to be functioning alcoholics with challenging and controlling behaviours, which only added to the turmoil. This left me without any positive male figure to look up to.

The absence of a father meant missing out on the love, support, and wisdom that a paternal figure could provide. I craved someone to teach me life's important lessons, to offer guidance during difficult times, and to be a role model worthy of admiration.

But instead, I found myself navigating through a stormy sea of toxic men with negative relationships, which was hardly the role model that I needed.

Interestingly, my mother told me that my father taught himself to read and write. He had worked as a gardener for over three decades for the local authority. He took care of the bowling greens, and when he passed away in 2014, the bowling team and all his family and friends attended his funeral to show their respects.

I had come to realise over the years that my father was softly spoken and kept mostly to himself, traits which I think I've inherited.

There was a local pub around the corner on the estate where I lived. TC's parents owned it, and I visited frequently to hang out. He was older than me, but we got along well.

I would often help with the chores around the pub, like 'bottling up' and tidying up the backyard. We had a lot of fun together playing in the huge store cupboard, pretending it was a campground with bed sheets as tents.

We watched a lot of movies too. Although I wasn't great at pool, we still played without having to put 50 pence in the slot because it was free for us.

Whilst at TC's, we watched a lot of movies. One particular movie that caught my attention was *Rocky III*. Sylvester Stallone played the part of a fictional character whose strength and determination inspired me.

In watching the *Rocky* movies, I discovered an unyielding hero who showcased resilience. As his underdog status morphed into championship material, so did my ability to believe in myself despite my hardships.

Rocky's triumphs became a source of inspiration for me, as they gave me hope during moments of uncertainty. The poster of Rocky hanging in my bedroom at a young age evoked courage and optimism within me because if he could do that, maybe I could too someday. However, I was young then and didn't know how to put it all into practice.

Growing up, I tried to be positive like Rocky, but the environment I was in was always difficult. It always seemed like I had a health problem nipping at my heels.

My ears constantly released discharge and smelled bad; my two front teeth protruded. I also had the issue of bed wetting. I had to contend with being in remedial classes at school, and I was considered 'slow'.

Expressing emotions verbally has always been problematic for me as a child and an adult, I tend to keep my feelings bottled up until they manifest as anger instead of trying to explain how I'm feeling.

This leads to outbursts that are disproportionate to the situation at hand and make matters worse for me and others. Throughout my life, I have hesitated to express what I want to say to others; this has caused me great frustration.

I have learnt, especially when I was younger, that it is better to 'close up' and not tell others how you really feel to prevent uncomfortable feelings. This is because, most of the time, I felt lost in the midst of the experiences happening around me.

I could barely see anything positive about my future. I felt disconnected from myself and others like I had no purpose or place. Whenever I tried to express myself, it felt like a jumbled mess of words that didn't make sense. I wanted desperately to be able to express my feelings without reservation as it happened, but I was unable to do so.

I found solace in music; it allowed me to tap into emotions that I thought were buried. Although its beauty is indescribable, words will never do justice to how incredibly powerful music can be for some people.

Music transcends language barriers and provides hope during moments of despair. It provided comfort when everything else seemed bleak and lifeless. Despite all this, sometimes I struggle to understand my innermost emotions.

It feels like an uphill battle, trying to make sense of all the chaos within my mind because all these feelings war against each other, making it difficult to comprehend what I'm feeling at any given moment.

However, every day is another opportunity for growth; every moment is another chance to find something new within me that brings me closer to understanding who I am and what I need in life for me to feel content.

Music has always been my refuge and escapism; however, I can't help but feel a deep sense of disconnection within myself. I am aware that my life experiences have shaped the way I deal with pain, emotion, and feelings in peculiar ways.

One moment, my mind can feel completely blank, like an endless void, an overwhelming wave that changes my entire state of being instantly. It could be frustration or detachment, but I feel disconnected from everyone else because no one understands me.

I even find it difficult to understand myself at times. Music makes me feel alive and connected to the world because it allows me to experience real emotions, reflect on past events and try to make sense of them, although I know I never will.

Sometimes, I feel like a robot mimicking the emotions I have observed instead of expressing them, almost like I am putting mechanisms in place. Despite this, I am grateful for the moments when music allows me to experience what it is like to truly feel alive.

I can understand that living in a family where violence and alcohol are present can build resentment and anger. These situations have left me wanting to be in control of things and not step outside of my comfort zone.

These are my problems, but I try to navigate them by taking 'time out' to unwind my head from all my experiences. I'm afraid to let other people see my true feelings. Being able to dance, laugh, and smile without reservations and losing my inhibitions feels just out of reach.

I feel shut off from myself and others and cannot truly let go and experience life in the moment. If I were honest with myself, I'd have to admit that instead of living through emotion, I'm merely imitating it, but I have become so good at it that I convince myself it is real.

Although I'm not familiar with the sensation, I understand the concept of love. I can use the word to describe what I feel on paper, but I'm uncertain if I can convey its meaning completely and accurately through conversation.

I had been contemplating if an Autism Spectrum Disorder (ASD) assessment could help me make sense of the way I think and my behaviour. I understand everyone experiences emotions differently, but I struggle to recognise empathy and can easily be overwhelmed by information and social cues.

It's challenging for me to express my feelings effectively, which can be quite frustrating at times. I have a diagnosis of dyslexia, which has implications for my daily activities, from how I feel to how I communicate, behave, and carry out my daily events.

It makes it harder for me to fit in with other people around me as well as to interact with them in meaningful ways. In addition, there are times when my brain is so overwhelmed by all the noise inside it that everything around me becomes a blur, and it takes me some time to regain my focus.

Sometimes, I compare my mind to a train on a track. There's a hitch that's preventing it from moving smoothly. To keep going, I need to fix the issue. My method is finding a peaceful place to sort through my thoughts and make sense of them. Once I've done that, I'm able to move forward again, just like the train on the track.

I can remember occasions where my mother expressed emotion towards me, but one situation stands out as being very awkward. It was when she was in the hospital for smoking-related complications in 2018.

I recall visiting the ward, knowing that my older siblings had all visited, hugged and kissed her on the cheek because that was their nature, and they are all quite tactile. I thought I would give my mother a hug whilst visiting her, but there was an uncomfortable attempt at me expressing emotion, which felt very clinical.

Without a word, I could feel my mother thinking, 'What are you doing?' I was not normally demonstrative like that, but I thought I would give it a try. It felt quite uncomfortable. I said goodbye, and the moment felt more detached and clinical rather than an expression of love towards a mother.

I believe we all come into this world with predisposed conditioning, which shapes how we interpret the world around us. As we grow and learn, our brains absorb information to condition us in certain ways of behaving.

Yet, some things elude us and go unnoticed, like hidden feelings buried deep within us, guarded by walls we construct each day. I spent a long time trying to uncover my own hidden emotions.

This is very difficult because when words can't express what I'm feeling, I don't know how to react or to say it verbally in a way that makes sense. This creates a block, and therefore, I become frustrated and tend to write my feelings down on paper to convey them, which I find is a more focused and calmer process that works for me.

Living in a hectic home environment puts pressure on my character and how I feel. The ever-present discord and drama drains me emotionally, leaving me feeling worn out and uneasy in a place that should be my haven.

The perpetual turbulence saps my resilience and resolve, making it harder for me to stay in a high mood. It is difficult to rise above an environment that, in my early years, could have been perceived as negative due to circumstances.

I guess the positive is that I have become more understanding and compassionate towards others due to this experience, as I can relate to the difficulties others might be facing.

On the flip side, it can sometimes leave me feeling overwhelmed and emotionally drained, making me more guarded and closed off in an attempt to protect myself. The experiences have been enormously demanding and have moulded me significantly.

The frequent commotion and lack of steadiness have had a profound impact on my joy, social life, and personal growth.

One of the most noticeable outcomes of living in a difficult environment is its effect on my cheerfulness. Being surrounded by arguments, tension, and insecurity produces an unrelenting feeling of unease.

It's hard to be content and appreciate life when the mood is always one of tension. The recurrent emotional pandemonium leaves me drained, making it difficult to keep positive feelings alive.

The instability at home has also profoundly changed how I view myself. Building a strong, secure identity is difficult when the world around me is so unstable and without a structure.

A direction of just knowing is important, which can aid in the future. A lack of support and the tools to navigate through life can also be tough in managing the hardships of growing up and discovering who I truly am.

Having to constantly adjust to fluxing dynamics leaves me feeling confused and uncertain about my place in this world. This was due to hopping from one situation to the next. Despite these difficulties, I've also learnt valuable lessons from growing up in such an environment.

It has taught me resilience, resourcefulness, and the importance of self-reliance, as in not relying on anyone. I've had to develop a strong sense of independence and learn to rely on myself for stability and emotional support.

By remaining aware of my strength born of trials and tribulations, I will be better able to continue striving onwards towards personal development and contentment.

Chapter 2
Rivalry

As I dive into this chapter, I am faced with the difficult task of addressing and letting go of emotions that have long lingered within me. Feelings of frustration and anger that I've held onto for far too long.

On top of that, there is also a sense of uncertainty as I am unsure how my words will be received by others. My ultimate goal is for this to serve as a learning experience for all involved rather than causing further tension.

Perhaps there are other families and situations out there that are just waiting for a push or an opportunity to heal and become whole again.

The relentless competition, green-tinged jealousy, and heated conflict between siblings can be a treacherous minefield to navigate. A natural occurrence born from a deep-seated desire for attention, resources, and parental affection.

The rivalry is often fuelled by an unquenchable need to outdo one another in academics or sports, to gain their parents' favour, or even to claim ownership over personal belongings and personal space.

Whilst a healthy dose of competition can be beneficial for individual growth, this constant struggle for dominance can also create deep rifts within the familial unit, threatening to shatter the bonds of kinship.

Bickering between siblings can be seen as a normal part of behaviour growing up. But from my experience, it felt like there was something different that made this difficult to cope with physically and mentally.

I also think that it surpassed 'normal' sibling rivalry. The memory of countless situations has always been in the back of my mind, although it has lessened over time. However, you know it's there, buried in the depths of your subconscious; like any experience in life, it stays with you.

I thought about it constantly when I was younger and as an adult. I still, at times, am unable to shake the feeling of the experiences throughout my childhood.

I don't believe I was particularly close with anyone when thinking about my own experiences of living at home. I believe this may be a common theme with me. However, over the years, I believe that a bond can get stronger as you get older, depending on the status of the relationship.

I like to think that I have a deeper understanding and appreciation for most things. But back then, I was always at odds, whether it was over personal items, ideas, or views. Even though there were childish rivalries, I felt that they were taken too far.

There seemed to be resentment in the air, which made me, in turn, feel hatred within. I feel that rivalry will always be a factor in any relationship, let alone within a family. I have often spoken about my account of events, and it is difficult to relate it to 'typical behaviour'.

My own recollection of those moments is far different, and in my mind, there was more to it. My mother would occasionally go out for the night. At times, I felt like I couldn't just relax, having to be in an environment I did not want to be in and just wanting to be on my own.

No matter how much I wanted to leave, there always seemed to be something blocking me, which impacted my ability to go because I just wanted peace. The feeling of being confined in any space seemed like it stayed with me forever.

This is probably why I don't like the feeling of being in small spaces. I felt that there were times I was unable to get away, having no control and desperate to remove myself from any given situation.

I often wondered if certain situations were caused by me. I am not sure what I had done or said, but thinking about it now, I guess it may have been because I was 'different', which has always played a part in my life. I also felt that no one understood me.

When everyone went out, and I was left in solitude, I relished the fleeting moments of peace. But these moments were very short lived. With each passing minute, I clung to my solitude like a precious gem, for it was the only time that truly belonged to me.

The only sounds were the satisfying hiss of my cold Cola opening and the satisfying crunch of my crisps between my teeth. My gaze was fixed on the TV screen, where Condor Man, played by the talented Michael Crawford, took flight. It's no wonder I still find comfort in being alone—it's my brief escape from the chaos of the outside world.

It's hard for me to explain or understand why people act in such ways or what inspires outbursts of anger, control, or dominance. It's almost as if feelings of frustration were present. Whatever the cause of the behaviour, it impacted me considerably.

As an adult, I often wonder if any deep-seated issues were present. I never delved into it due to a lack of resources or external help. I believe this could have provided insight into the situation; plus, at the time, being young, I did not know how to navigate all of this.

As a child, all I wanted was to have friends and be accepted by my peers. So, whenever I was invited to join a group of friends, I eagerly accepted.

However, instead of being embraced, I was met with comments about my appearance, something I was already extremely self-conscious about. Looking back, perhaps these individuals were acting out to hide their own inner turmoil or insecurities.

On the outside, I always seemed to be in control of my emotions. I would laugh off any insults thrown at me and ignore what was hurting me inside. But I was slowly crumbling under the weight of insults and put-downs.

I know the power of words and what they can do and this at times was not really understood. The impact they would have on a person can be lasting. But I wished there had been more of an awareness of how much I was affected. All I ever wanted to do was to fit in with everyone around me, but instead of being accepted, I felt very different.

I tried to find solace in things like music and computers, which brought joy to my life. It wasn't easy trying to maintain a strong face whilst still dealing with all the emotional turmoil that came with having such a difficult childhood.

That's why it's important for children everywhere who are still facing similar issues today to have access to resources that can help them learn how to cope with these types of situations healthily in order for them to move forward into their future without any lasting trauma or damage.

As I've grown older, I've realised just how difficult forgiveness can be, and even more so when trying to articulate one's feelings about a past experience.

But for a long time, I have learnt to push those memories and experiences to the back of my mind and work on letting go of all the anger and frustration that has consumed me for so long.

I've never been completely honest with myself about how these moments affected me. I feel that writing these words down is a necessary step in releasing myself from this grip and moving forward, in the sense of learning not to be angry or be consumed by endless thoughts.

Chapter 3
Overwhelming

I had never thought something so shocking would happen to me; I was just a kid, after all. I had been playing near our house when a car pulled up beside me; the woman inside the car said that she was from the Education Welfare Office and asked why I wasn't at school.

She offered to drive me back to school. Naively, I accepted a ride from the woman. Little did I know that the woman would lead me to some abandoned garages and not to school. I was treated inhumanely for hours.

She demanded I dance with charcoal smeared on my face. Fortunately, I managed to fight back by kicking her in her private parts, giving me enough time to escape. I returned home, and my mother took immediate action.

She sent me to sit near the windowsill and stare out the window at the main road to watch for them in case she came back. Miraculously, I spotted her, and it was reported back to my mother, leading to justice being served.

Years had crawled by, each one leaving me with profound memories from my previous abduction. But just when I thought I had endured the worst, fate twisted and delivered me to a new level of agony and terror.

My memories of that time are blurred, but the stench of Surrey Docks—now known as Surrey Quays still lingers in my mind.

Without warning, a pack of men descended upon me and pulled me into a decrepit, what looked like a shed, where they unleashed their brutality upon me without remorse. I have a vague vison of fists being pounded on my body until it was bruised, whilst their sickening acts, like urinating on me, left me feeling violated and degraded.

As I lay there, trapped in this living nightmare, I couldn't fathom why this torment was being inflicted upon me. It was confusing, and there seemed to be no escape from its clutches, apart from walking off afterwards, confused and dazed.

Social Services

Social workers played a significant role in my life. I can recall the cold, sterile environment of the Southwark Council Social Services Office, where we received handouts. The first thing that struck me about the office was its lack of warmth and humanity.

However, the social workers did offer us support in other ways, providing vouchers. Despite feeling embarrassed and ashamed about our situation, I am grateful for their assistance, as it truly made a difference for us.

It is ironic that I became a social worker myself, addressing the very issues and experiences I encountered as a child but with adults. Perhaps my own experiences have drawn me to this field, with a deep desire to help others going through similar struggles.

The Children's Camping Holiday Fund

I can vaguely remember my stomach feeling twisted as I waited for my train at the Paddington station, wearing a name badge and feeling somewhat lost. An adult was there to supervise a group of us, but I still felt abandoned.

Social Services had arranged for me to go on an ill-fated holiday to Cheshire to stay with some unfamiliar and unknown family. I remember at the time celebrations were going on because of Charles and Diana's wedding.

This was because, at the time, my mother could not afford for us to go anywhere, and I guess she also needed a break from us.

It was called the 'Children's Camping Holiday Fund', although it is now called the 'Holiday Activities and Food Programme', which is for school-aged children from reception to year 11 (inclusive) who receive benefits-related free school meals.

Despite the fanfare, I couldn't help but feel overwhelmed by sadness. There were arguments within that family that I stayed with, bearing in mind I didn't know them, and that made me nervous.

The loneliness filled me until it was time to return home. It was almost like being evacuated and having to live in an unknown place. But even returning home was not a positive experience.

Chapter 4
J. P. T.

The memories of my mother's partner's, in particular J, are clouded by the constant presence of alcohol. Like a dark cloud looming over our household, his drunkenness seemed to be a common theme.

I can picture one particular night in the front room, with its walls adorned with coloured lights that pulsed and changed with the rhythm of the TV's audio.

It was a mesmerising sight, especially on this revolutionary TV that had just been introduced at the time. Despite the chaos and toxicity that often surrounded us, I couldn't help but feel a sense of wonder and excitement at that moment.

I recall a machete hanging above the fireplace, its purpose and origin unknown. Suddenly, J stood up and snatched it from its place. My heart raced as he brandished the weapon, his anger palpable.

He took out his rage by smashing the television and tossing the knife across the room towards our cat. This was a common occurrence in our household. Violence, both physical and emotional, were not uncommon spectacles.

Every day, I would go to school with dread in my stomach, only to return home to more tension and fear at night.

Living amidst chaos created a sense of instability and unpredictability, making it difficult to find stability and peace. Witnessing violence and experiencing bullying led to feelings of fear, helplessness, and a distorted sense of self-worth.

The walls of my home echoed with angry shouting. It was a place where love was scarce, replaced by fear and uncertainty. Each day, I watched as my mother's boyfriend devoured hopes and aspirations by unleashing violence.

I still remember the sickening feeling in my stomach as I came home from school one day, the unmistakable stench of excrement permeating the air after opening the front door. It was on the floor in the toilet, a stark reminder of my mother's boyfriend's drunkenness and the inability to control their essential functions.

Even after coming back from our first family holiday to Spain, I was happy, but not with J, as things didn't improve. I can still recall walking up to our front door, hesitant and unsure of what was waiting inside.

The moment J answered the door, an overpowering wave of excrement odour hit me square in the face, nearly knocking me off my feet. In the days that followed, J's temper would only worsen, and he'd lash out at my mother with violent fury, giving her two black eyes and sometimes beating her with chains.

On many occasions, she hid behind sunglasses. This cycle of abuse continued for years on end, and I felt like our house was a cursed place, off-limits to visitors and outsiders alike lest they discover the horrors brewing within.

Over time, a strange transition appeared in the house. Unknowingly, this man was going to be my mother's next partner. I had seen a man called P who occasionally visited my mother.

P got J to leave; well, he threw him out because of his behaviour. I remember looking out of my bedroom window as I could see the front balcony below.

One thing that stands out about me is that I have developed an innate sense of tidiness. I am not sure who I took after, but I would make sure my bedroom was kept in order and neat.

This behaviour became a way for me to find solace amidst the chaotic environment I was living in. When I organised a space, it allowed me to find control in an otherwise uncontrollable situation.

During my teenage years, I had my own portable radio placed on my windowsill and would often listen to Radio Luxembourg's Top 40 show under the covers late at night. It was a chance for me to escape from reality and feel liberated by music, even if it meant having to sneak around so I would not get caught listening to it because I should have been sleeping.

Regardless of all the trauma surrounding my upbringing, one thing that has always stayed with me is this sense of organisation, which I developed as a coping strategy during my teenage years.

Even now, being able to organise spaces gives me comfort and security during difficult times. Despite all the chaos that surrounded me growing up, organising my environment provides me with moments in which I can find peace.

From my balcony, I remember seeing some sort of altercation between P and J. I then realised that J had left and P, as strange as it sounds, 'took over'. It was then that he replaced J as my mother's partner.

One bonus, I would say, at the time, is that P did not appear to be a drinker. However, he was something else that would further impact all our lives. However, it appeared to be a relaxed environment without J.

I guess you could say which is the lesser of two evils. I think any situation would have been better than dealing with J's violence, drunkenness, and disgusting behaviour. Many years later, my sibling shared the news with me that J had died of an alcohol-related illness. I felt no remorse and was glad such a parasite had left this earth.

When J left, and P came into our lives, I did not yet understand the dynamics of what was happening. There didn't seem to be anything wrong with P, from what I could see. He was younger than my mother and treated us better than her previous partner.

We no longer lived in fear or had that stench coming from inside the house. Although J had been thrown out, there was something else. P was a petty criminal who was always doing bits and pieces to make money.

Small things become big things. I guess one bonus is that he did give us money for school and provided us with clothes and food on the table. But the environment went from one extreme to the next.

Things were looking up, and everything was going well. I lived with no violence, drunkenness, or intimidation as I had done with J. But thinking about it now, nothing lasts forever. It was not long before P would carry out burglaries, rent televisions from rental providers and then sell them for a profit.

My mother was cutting cheques and ordering goods from a catalogue from one address and then moving them to another. She would then sell the goods.

My mother worked together with P; I guess you could call them 'partners in crime'. My mother felt that she could trust P; after all, she finally didn't have someone around who knocked her about.

I believe she finally found someone to share her life with. But you can never tell who is really there to help you until it's too late.

P lived with us for quite a while. His presence was palpable, but his purpose was unclear. My mother fell pregnant in 1987 with twins. Despite these circumstances, P remained present throughout the birth.

I remember visiting my mother at Greenwich Hospital and thinking that he seemed to be around for quite some time. But remember, I said nothing lasts forever.

Inevitably, P carried on with his illegal ways, desperate to make money by any means necessary. Things changed from one extreme to another as he attempted an armed robbery shortly after the twins had been born.

He was caught and held accountable for his actions. He attended the Old Bailey, where he was sentenced to approximately eight years in prison. Life soon took a turn for the worse.

My mother, along with all of us, then spent countless hours visiting various prisons whilst growing up, trying to maintain a relationship with P despite his incarceration.

The day P was released after being in prison for so many years, he was a changed man. He had slipped into criminality again and carried out various bits and pieces to make money.

On one occasion, he had been deported from the UK due to his criminal behaviour, and my mother hadn't heard from him for months. He never moved back with us or took an interest in my younger siblings. He would disappear from their lives just as fast as he entered them.

I moved out of the house some time ago, which is another story. But as soon as you think someone has gone, they will come back to disrupt and upset the balance.

I had visited my mother regularly whilst she was at home. She was bringing up my younger brother and sister on her own. On one particular day, I visited my mother and was shocked that P was present and had visited the house, albeit he had been away for a very long time.

There was also another man in the house called T. To my knowledge, P was no longer involved with my mother. From what I was told at the time, P and T were friends. When I walked into the kitchen, my mother introduced me to T, who had recently come to London.

Although I did not handle it well, my mother told me that T is now living in the house. This information came as a shock to me because P was sitting right there in the kitchen with them. This left me feeling awkward about being inside the home.

Yet, my mother sat next to T comfortably as if nothing was wrong. I stormed out of the house and did not talk to my mother for quite some time.

After some time, I started to visit my mother again. But as I got to observe and see T, it was evident that he was just another functioning alcoholic. He would try and hide it, but after having experiences of living with previous drinkers, you just know what to look out for.

Over the years, my mother told me that when T got drunk, he would psychologically abuse her, but she did not want me to do anything about it.

I remember being told that he would hide things from my mother; she would then look for them, and he would put them back for the purpose of making her feel that she was losing her mind.

My mother's bedroom had become a dumping ground for T's beer cans and cigarettes. I was aware that the bedroom had not been decorated for at least 20 years. My mother had always taken pride in her home and care of herself until these people came into her life.

They made her prioritise the needs of others over her own, leading to a steady deterioration of not just her house but also her well-being. It's truly heart-breaking.

When I reminisce on my years living at home and visiting often, I can see my mother in my mind's eye. She was always putting her heart into polishing, tidying up and making sure the house was spotless. It brought her peace and joy.

Yet, as time moved forward, some bad moves and life events seemed to push her to a brink where she could no longer take care of her mental and psychological state. Despite her struggles, my mother tried to always appear fine and in control.

But deep down, I could tell she was putting on a brave face. The home that had once been perfectly orderly and clean seemed to be taken over by the people who kept coming in and out of her life. My mother seemed unable to take back control until, eventually, it felt like she'd just ceded authority altogether.

I felt a profound sadness seeing my mother sink further into depression, and the home gradually fell apart. I remembered a time when the house was immaculate, reflecting her indomitable spirit.

But life had taken its toll on her, and it seemed that she couldn't bear the burden of her suffering any longer. The thought of these men taking advantage of my mother's gentle nature and exploiting her psychologically makes my stomach ache. Having to witness this experience has been devastating, so I wanted to tell the story from my point of view.

Throughout my mum's life, she has had partners' who have used her vulnerability and kindness to their advantage. Their choices gradually eroded her emotional well-being, leaving her feeling exhausted and emotionally drained.

They seemed to be making calculated decisions with the intention of controlling my mother's life through a sea of alcohol, disruption, and emotional and psychological behaviour.

At first, I would guess that these men may have been charming and caring, but that changed with time. They began to exhibit behaviour that was damaging my mother's confidence and self-worth. Their choices were always focused on themselves, disregarding my mother's feelings and needs.

The worse decisions there were, the harder life became for my mother; it felt like her spirit was becoming duller. She found herself stuck in a cycle of emotional struggles as she searched for love and acceptance from these partners.

Eventually, their actions eroded her self-esteem and left her exhausted and questioning her own value.

I witnessed my mother's spirit gradually diminish, replaced by uncertainty in her life. It was heart-breaking to observe her immersing herself in hurtful relationships, placing her well-being aside for the benefit of someone who was only causing her harm. She seemed to be unable to liberate herself from this draining situation, entangled in a web of control and deceit.

My mother passed away in March 2018 as a result of her smoking. I was at work when it happened. I was told she had gone upstairs, laid down in her bed, and passed away. It's like she knew this would be the end for her.

She had lots of hopes and dreams that were never realised; those around her took advantage of her in such a way that it always seemed her own life was secondary to everyone else's. It's such a tragedy that her aspirations never saw the light of day.

My mother had passed away, and whilst her personal belongings were being handled with care, I was told that a diary had been discovered that held the phrase 'not happy' written down on the days of the week.

My heart plummeted as I considered all she must have gone through, trying to put up a brave front despite all her pain. Knowing that she kept it all inside only highlighted the fact that passing away was her only way of escaping the misery and finding rest. It seemed smoking was the only time she let herself be truly content and in control.

The biggest sorrow in my life is that my mother never got to experience what she truly desired. She could have had so much joy, and it's truly heart-breaking that she could not get the chance to pursue her dreams.

J, P, and T, all tragically passed away due to the destructive effects of alcohol on their bodies. Despite their individual differences, they shared a common fate brought about by their heavy drinking habits.

It was a heart-breaking loss that left a void in the lives of those who knew and loved them, something I could never feel towards any of them.

Chapter 5
Hospital Admissions

As a young child, I was admitted to Guy's Hospital due to bed wetting. I remember being on the very top floor, and it seemed like a massive ward. I vaguely remember a man coming to meet and talk with me once a week.

Thinking about it now as I'm older, he may have been a psychiatrist, perhaps talking through my difficulties, etc. I think the bed wetting was because of the worry I had to endure in life, i.e. the stress because of my mother's boyfriends and being at home.

I didn't have a say or a view about it at the time. I don't think I was even allowed to go out on my own, even out of the ward. It felt like I stayed there for months upon months. My days intermingled with one another.

It felt like what should have been Christmas time became winter, and what should have been summer holidays was replaced by long nights.

My mother came to see me on Wednesdays to take part in baking with me at the hospital. I remember one visit; my mother brought in an A-Team annual book for me to read. The hospital staff would take me and others to an adventure playground trip every Monday.

The hospital staff also provided swimming lessons. I recall being allowed to partake in an Easter egg hunt. Each Thursday, I was able to immerse myself and escape the reality of my situation by watching Top of the Pops at 7 pm in the communal room. I guess that is also a reason why I love listening to music so much.

Whilst at the hospital, I remember one evening, I awoke from a deep sleep. My ears were filled with a shrill ringing sound. I was told by a nurse who had come over to me, "You have wet the bed."

I remember there was a metal grid under my hospital-issued bed and mattress. This made a very loud buzzing sound after it detected urine. This meant that everyone knew that I had wet the bed.

Every morning I woke up, I would pull myself out of bed. My legs were tangled in sheets drenched with urine. I recall the nurse helping me with my clothes and changing the bedding.

Looking back, I feel that my dignity was affected by the whole experience of knowing about my incontinence and requiring me to get up and change in front of them. Knowing what had just happened shrank my self-esteem, although I was too young to really think about the ramifications and the effect that it would all have on me.

I remember coming home from the hospital at the weekend, but this was counterproductive, as the home environment would be chaotic. It would have been safe to leave me in the ward so I did not have to endure the chaotic situations of being at home.

I was happy to return to the hospital but equally sad because of the very nature I was in the hospital. I remember after such time coming home from hospital and bringing a friend to my house. I now realise that was not a good idea.

My room smelled of urine because of my bed wetting. The so-called 'friend' then told people in school that my room smelled of wee. I was then known as the kid who smelled of wee and was teased relentlessly.

I remember being in the changing room at school and seeing all those eyes turned towards me, looking in disgust. I would sit there, undressing, fumbling to get my PE kit on, whilst everyone would stare at me because my legs were red due to the urine soaking in my skin, which looked cracked and sore.

This became easily noticeable by the others. I can vaguely recall being bathed and standing up in either a sink or a bathtub from when I was a child. The odour of urine just seemed to linger around me and there were red patches on my legs that I noticed.

At the time, I had no recollection of agreeing to be admitted to the hospital or what would take place; although I was under 18, a conversation still would have been nice. I wasn't given permission to leave unless someone else went with me.

Even though I was old enough to move around and not leave the ward, I wasn't allowed to venture outside its walls or out of the hospital. From my point of view, the recurrent misfortune of bedwetting has been an ample source of frustration and embarrassment throughout my life.

The ramifications of this involuntary act have presented a multitude of challenges that have left me feeling alone and misunderstood both physically and emotionally.

The physical act of bedwetting was unbearable and degrading. Waking up to a damp bed was both disturbing and tiring, leaving me feeling worn out and unsettled. The continuous necessity to change the sheets added extra difficulty to my everyday schedule, making me feel as if I was in a constant struggle with myself.

Bedwetting had a significant impact on how I felt about myself. The worry that someone would find out or make fun of me caused me to avoid making social connections and going to sleepovers.

The shame I experienced due to this condition made me more reclusive and scared of being called 'abnormal' by others. The bedwetting has definitely had a psychological effect on me, making me doubt my abilities and feeling inadequate. It can be hard to stay confident when you're faced with the same issue again and again.

The sudden ending of my bedwetting problem in my late teens was a significant and freeing event that gave me great comfort and reinvigorated my self-esteem. After having difficulties with this involuntary action for ages, the unexpected transition created a big transformation in my life.

Suddenly, the pressure to stay dry had disappeared, and I could finally breathe without fear of embarrassment or judgment.

Chapter 6
My School Days

I have very negative memories and emotions of my primary and secondary school. I think I blocked some of it out. But what I do know is that being different played a substantial part in making me feel isolated from school, as well as having no friends and even feeling isolated overall.

Being different in the sense that I was constantly seen as 'slow' or 'stupid'. I was made to feel that I would achieve nothing and was made to feel like the odd one out. This was a view that even extended family members had. I associate school with bullying, unhappiness and a darkness that pervades my feelings and thoughts.

Every time I left primary school at the end of the day, a sense of dread would wash over me. I knew that the usual suspects would be waiting for me and lurking around. I even remember their names.

It had become a routine, a cruel game I couldn't escape. As soon as I bolted out of the school gates, they would pounce, inflicting their torment upon me. I always remember running home, but I was never fast enough.

It pains me why human beings can be so harsh. I've never hurt anyone, yet only because of my appearance and character

I was a target, something I still struggle to comprehend even now.

The memories of those names still haunt me to this day. The bullies who seemed to relish in my misery, their faces etched in my mind like scars. Each encounter left me battered and bruised, physically and emotionally. It felt like I was trapped in a cycle of torment, unable to break free.

In those moments, it seemed as though everyone around me had built walls, shutting me out from their world. I was an outsider, unwanted and invisible. Their indifference pierced my heart, reminding me of my loneliness.

And there, tucked behind my ear, was the clear plastic shell of my hearing aid, a constant companion. It amplified the sounds from the outside world, a reminder of the unique challenges I faced.

I still remember the day as if it had happened just yesterday. I was in the playground at school, lost in my own thoughts when suddenly, someone came up from behind me and delivered a powerful blow to my ear that had the hearing aid in it.

The impact reverberated through my bones, and an intense surge of pain engulfed my head. It was as if my world had been shattered in an instant. As the pain wracked my body, I felt a warm sensation trickling down my neck.

Confusion washed over me, and I couldn't comprehend why I was bleeding. The sight of people around me, laughing and enjoying the spectacle, only deepened my distress. I desperately wanted to ask someone what had happened, to seek solace or understanding, but my voice failed me.

That incident marked a turning point in my relationship with hearing aids. It instilled in me a deep-seated fear and hesitation. The very devices that were meant to help me hear became a source of anxiety and discomfort.

Every time I put on a hearing aid, it serves as a reminder of that painful moment, a constant trigger for the lingering trauma.

At that same primary school, I recall the humiliation of being called fleabag and being told I smelled of wee and being called 'wet the bed'. The other kids said I was a freak, and they teased me about wearing a hearing aid.

I vaguely remember on one occasion, the headmaster of the primary school I attended called my sibling into the office. The headmaster then expressed that I smelled of wee in front of them.

I remember always having a wash in the morning, but where I would lay in my own urine after wetting the bed, my skin would be all red, and it was hard to be completely clean and odour-free.

It was a struggle to make friends in school. I was always the quiet one. The one who preferred to stay within their own comfort zone of familiarity. I never felt attractive or confident enough to converse freely with others.

Every day, I would come home from school exhausted and defeated after facing yet another day of judgment and ridicule.

The remedial classes were the worst for me. I quickly learnt that my hearing aids made me different from my peers, and it only increased my feelings of isolation and exclusion.

The lessons were difficult to understand, and I often found myself struggling to keep up with the material being taught. Inevitably, this would lead to further criticism and humiliation from my peers when they noticed my confusion and inability to comprehend.

I found solace in tinkering and taking things apart and putting them back together. My mind was always racing, trying to make sense of my experiences and why I felt so different.

It wasn't until much later in life, as an adult, that I was diagnosed with dyslexia in 2009 and autism in 2023. In the '70s and '80s, they were not well known or understood, so people like me were simply labelled as 'different' or having something 'wrong' with me.

Looking back, I realise there was nothing wrong with me; I just had a unique wiring that required support on my level instead of trying to fit into the mould of a 'normal' typical child. Unfortunately, this understanding was lacking during my childhood.

The only support offered was placing me in remedial classes, which did not address my needs. I even remember being forced to write with my right-hand despite being left-handed.

There was no effort made to explore my individual needs; instead, I was simply labelled as a 'special' child. This inadvertently drew attention to me that resulted in being bullied.

The most prominent memories I have from school are feeling alone, being teased, criticised, and socially excluded. All of these experiences took their toll on my self-esteem and sense of worth as a person.

On some mornings, even before leaving for school, I would find myself wanting to cry because I did not want to go back there anymore, back into an environment where no one understood or accepted me for who I was.

Throughout my school years, there was one subject that caused me the most anxiety and self-doubt, which was maths. From a young age, I struggled to understand the concepts and equations, and the more I fell behind, the more discouraged I became.

I vividly remember one particular day in class when my math teacher decided to call on me to solve an addition problem on the board. My heart started racing as soon as I heard my name being called.

All eyes were on me as I walked up to the board, feeling like a deer caught in headlights. The pressure to perform was overwhelming, and I could feel myself getting hotter and hotter with embarrassment.

As I tried to solve the problem, my mind went blank. The numbers started to blur together, and all I could hear were muffled laughs coming from some of my classmates. Tears welled up in my eyes as I felt like a failure once again.

Looking back now, I can see that this single moment had a significant impact on how I viewed myself as a learner. It reinforced the belief that I was not good enough or smart enough to understand maths. And from that day on, every time we had a maths lesson, my anxiety would skyrocket.

It didn't help that, alongside struggling with maths, I also had learning difficulties that made it even more challenging for me to grasp the subject. But instead of receiving support and understanding from my teachers and peers, all I received was criticism and mockery.

My self-esteem took a hit each time I failed to solve a problem or understand a concept. It felt like no matter how hard I studied or practised at home; it would never be good enough in class.

I often wonder what impact this experience would have had on me if someone had taken the time to explain things in a way that made sense or showed patience and kindness towards me instead of bullying and ridicule.

Maybe then, math wouldn't be such an intimidating subject for me, and my confidence in my abilities would be stronger.

I dreaded the yearly cross-country running event. As a child, I struggled with bedwetting, which resulted in my legs being constantly cracked, dry and sore from the urine that would soak into my skin overnight.

I was embarrassed and ashamed of this condition, and it only added to the anxiety I felt about participating in physical activities.

I had no choice but to attend the event. There were no single cubicles or showering facilities available back then, so changing on my own was not an option. I would have to face the other pupils in my P.E. kit with my red and irritated legs on full display.

I remember one particular pupil who would always look at me in disgust and make cruel remarks about my appearance. They teased me relentlessly, pointing out my bedwetting issue and any other flaws they could find. It felt like they took great pleasure in making me feel small and inadequate.

During these events, all I wanted to do was run away and be alone forever. I didn't want anyone to see me or judge me for something that was beyond my control. It seemed like no matter how hard I tried to fit in or be accepted, there was always someone ready to tear me down.

Looking back now, I realise how much this experience affected my self-esteem and confidence. The constant teasing and ridicule made me feel like an outsider, like there was something fundamentally wrong with me that made me unworthy of acceptance.

It took a toll on my mental health and made me retreat further into myself. I often wonder what impact it would have had if someone had stood up for me or shown compassion towards me instead of joining in on the bullying.

Maybe then, I wouldn't have felt so alone and isolated during these events. But unfortunately, that wasn't the case for most of my school years.

As I grew older, my experiences with bullying and exclusion continued to impact me in various aspects of my life. One recurring fear that I still carry with me today is the fear of not being chosen or accepted by others. This fear has had a significant impact on my participation in physical activities and group events.

I remember joining a gym as an adult, however, as soon as classes were announced or team workouts were mentioned, I would immediately feel anxious and nervous. My biggest fear was not being chosen by other participants.

It reminded me of how I was always the last one standing during school sports events, waiting, and hoping for someone to pick me for their team. But it rarely happened, and when it did, it felt more like pity than genuine acceptance.

This fear led me to avoid group workouts and instead opt for solo classes or exercises alone at home. Even when attending group classes like 'circuit', I would always stay towards the back of the room, afraid of being noticed or judged by others.

It's incredible how one experience can have such a lasting effect on our psyche. It's been years since those school events, but that feeling of not being good enough or worthy enough to be chosen still haunts me.

It's a constant battle between wanting to participate and pushing myself out of my comfort zone, whilst also fearing rejection and judgement from others.

I often wonder if those experiences had been different and if I would feel more confident in group settings now. Maybe then, I wouldn't hesitate to join a team workout or attend group fitness classes without worrying about being picked last or not fitting in.

But unfortunately, those memories are still ingrained in my mind and continue to affect my self-esteem and confidence. It's something I continue to work on.

As someone who has experienced bullying both as a child and in my teens, at home and in school, I can attest to the profound and lasting negative effects it can have on an individual's life.

The scars left by bullying run deep, impacting not only my self-esteem but also my emotional well-being and overall quality of life. As a child, bullying was a relentless force that hovered over me every day.

The constant name-calling, insults, and physical aggression made me feel small, powerless, and unworthy. It chipped away at my self-confidence, leaving me questioning my own worth and struggling to find my place in the world. The emotional pain was overwhelming, and it often felt like there was no escape.

The impacts of bullying can extend far beyond those formative years. Even as I grew older, the memories and insecurities lingered, affecting my interactions with others and my ability to trust.

It created a sense of hypervigilance, always on guard for potential threats or judgment. The emotional wounds from childhood bullying shaped my self-perception, leading to self-doubt and a constant fear of rejection.

As an adult, I find myself struggling with hearing aids. The psychological wounds from that incident in the playground have left a lasting impact. It takes immense effort to overcome the fears and doubts that have taken root within me.

But I am determined not to let those experiences define me. I am gradually learning to navigate the challenges, seeking support, and understanding along the way. Though the road may be difficult, I refuse to let the actions of these people dictate my relationship with hearing aids. I strive to reclaim my autonomy.

Chapter 7
Why

It's often a struggle not to let go of the thoughts and judgments others may have of me, or even my own thoughts about myself, because we all want to be accepted. I carry the weight of assumptions made about me to the point where it consumes my every thought.

I admire those who speak their mind with confidence, without fear of judgment or backlash. Most of my life has been spent fixating on others' opinions of me rather than focusing on myself. I'm not sure exactly where this tendency comes from, but I can only assume it stems from childhood experiences.

I was always careful to avoid any confrontations or uncomfortable situations that would cause me harm or upset. However, I often suppressed my feelings, and they would eventually manifest in passive-aggressive behaviour without addressing the root cause.

Unfortunately, this is still something that affects me as an adult. I've described it as carrying a hidden spectrum within me, much like Bruce Banner, who transforms into the Incredible Hulk when he becomes angry.

But unlike him, I don't turn into a powerful being when I'm angry; instead, I carry this range of emotions with me constantly. To manage it, I keep myself busy with activities that capture my interest and occupy my mind.

My childhood and adult experiences have often been on my mind, and the hardest part is not having an outlet to release the built-up pressure. This has led me to be overly controlled in my behaviour, but I have found ways to manage it through my interests, focus, and structured routines.

However, I know that eventually, I will need to confront these unresolved issues. It's important for me to let others understand how their actions made me feel and why they affected me in certain ways.

One of life's greatest struggles is being able to offer advice based on our own experiences, yet not being able to follow that same advice ourselves.

It's difficult to accept when we are unable to find answers for unfortunate events, especially when the root cause issue is that they shouldn't have occurred in the first place. We spend all our time pondering the cause, yet we never reach a resolution.

This would be the closure I would be seeking; however, closure often gives us a sense of purpose or explanation, but it's possible that there may not be one. Maybe it simply is what it is, i.e. actions taken without any underlying significance.

In my opinion, self-awareness is crucial in navigating the world. We need to understand why we behave the way we do, but sometimes, it's not that easy. At any moment, I could become reserved, distant, quiet, annoyed, or passive-aggressive.

And for a while, I would question myself and wonder what was causing these emotions. I would feel guilty about my behaviour and how it affects those around me.

I often wonder why I feel so irritated by those who seem to have everything handed to them on a silver platter; total care from their parents, wealth, endless opportunities, and a clear path for the future.

My own future was never set in stone, opportunities were scarce, and any progress made was mainly due to my own efforts, with a little help along the way. It's easy to feel envious, regretful, and resentful in comparison.

Unless we control those feelings, they will be a catalyst to not moving forward. Breaking out of a pattern, in my experience, is the hardest thing to do. You can be aware of it and know why it's happening, but still, you do it.

The memoirs I have written were to get everything out of my head, in the open and understand it from that perspective rather than letting it stagnate in my head.

Chapter 8
Family Values

Our lives are often intertwined with those of our relatives, even from the very beginning. Family members tend to have their own perceptions of us and try to insert themselves into our lives, believing they are helping us but sometimes making negative comments about our choices.

I had an uncle who is sadly no longer with us. He used to come around to my house and impose his life experiences on me instead of allowing me to form my own. It felt like I was a project, someone he wanted to 'fix' or guide in organising my life.

There are moments of discussion about whether turning off a light switch would cause more electricity. Also, if I am able to budget for shopping, look after myself or even my wife and kids.

As I mentioned before, my family members have a tendency to project their own expectations, beliefs, and their perception of me. This was especially evident when I gained the sponsorship to train as a social worker in 2009.

The response from one of my relatives was, "You must be the oldest person in the university." It seemed like they couldn't fathom the idea of someone my age pursuing a new career path at the age of 39, or they thought I did not have the brain power to actually see it through.

There was also another incident where a family member visited to say hello and for a cup of tea. They saw a car parked in my driveway and asked if it was mine. When I responded yes, I could see from their facial expression, they were so surprised by it.

It felt like they had this preconceived notion that I was not capable of owning or driving a car, let alone passing a driving test.

These moments serve as a reminder that my extended family has always had a set idea about who I am, even as an adult. They still see me as the same child they knew growing up, 'slow' I assume with a 'global development delay' and expect me to fit into that bracket.

But as we grow, changes in life happen, and with any luck, we are not the same person we once were. We evolve over time with the right support in place.

It can be frustrating at times to constantly have to defend myself and prove that I am capable of making my own decisions and living my life on my terms. But ultimately, their opinions do not define me, and I have learnt to block out their comments and focus on living authentically.

In the end, our families may mean well, but it's important for us to remember that we are our own individuals with our own journeys and experiences. We should not let anyone else's perceptions limit us or hinder us from reaching our goals.

Chapter 9
The Move

I was around 12 years old when my mother decided to uproot us and move to a completely different part of Southeast London. I guess this was a good thing so I could start over; plus, the area that we lived in was considered rough.

This was the time that I lost my Star Wars C-3PO action figure, which I still miss. I was concerned about moving, but before I left, I was determined to give my primary school class a going-away present.

My mother had bought a ready-made cake for my class. I can vaguely remember when I brought the cake in, no one wanted it. It was a strange thing to happen. I guess it was because of me.

I felt my heart sink with every passing second when that happened. Even now, all these years later, I struggle to articulate what that moment meant to me.

We moved to the new area to get away from the hustle and bustle of our old neighbourhood. However, I soon realised this new area had plenty of its own problems. I was regularly pestered by local gangs around the area.

I was so desperate to stand up for myself against their intimidation, yet I lacked self-belief and was powerless in this department. I'd never been taught how to confront bullies, knowing only about fear and humiliation due to what I had gone through at home and in my previous school. After relocating, it seemed like nothing had changed; I was still being chased and beaten up.

On the first day of starting a new secondary school, I stepped into the halls of the drama class, where a wave of nerves flooded me. Everywhere I looked, there were others laughing and talking and having a good time, but despite the noise, an eerie quietness surrounded me.

No one said hello or acknowledged my presence. I remember feeling like a ghost when walking into the drama class. No one was talking or taking notice of my existence among the swarm of unfamiliar faces.

I couldn't help but remember my hair was slightly long and greasy. It was a constant reminder of my self-consciousness, adding to my already overwhelming sense of insecurity.

With my shy nature, it was challenging for me to reach out to people, so I remained mostly ignored, drifting through the class like a solitary figure.

I was blissfully unaware of the challenges that lay ahead. All I knew was the isolation and the longing for connection that weighed heavily on my heart.

Little did I realise that my journey through school would be marked not only by the absence of words but also by the struggles and triumphs that awaited me, more so like my previous primary school did.

Everyone had their place in the school, but like primary school, I didn't seem to fit in anywhere. As time passed, I felt lonelier than ever before. I tried making friends, but no one seemed interested in me, as I was not popular and did not look cool at all.

On the other hand, when my sibling came into the school, everyone was suddenly drawn to them. Girls were interested in giving attention. They had all the friends they could handle and were quite popular, whilst on the other side of the coin, I struggled to find any companionship at all. This made me feel even more isolated.

One day, I was sitting in my bedroom, bearing in mind I continued to have a problem with my ears. I realised an odd smell coming from my left ear.

Little did I know then, but this problem continued into my 20s, and it would turn out to be a diagnosis of suppurative otitis media, which had profound effects on my life in the years to come and stemmed from my childhood.

It would cause a hearing impairment in both ears and eventually lead to having two operations on each ear.

Whilst all these things were happening to me, I felt alone and empty. Despite the many people who surrounded me, I had no one to talk with or express my feelings. There was one moment in my teens when I was by myself in the bathroom and realised the only way out of this situation was to take my own life using the light pull cord.

My mind raced with thoughts of self-destruction, but I couldn't make myself take that step; call it nervousness, but I am thankful for that feeling. Every thought was full of despair and anguish, yet a tiny spark of hope kept me from going through with it.

But still, the depression won out, and I returned to the world that had hurt me so much. I guess that's why I don't experience emotion or empathy or have an emotional response to situations in a positive way.

After struggling with school and the continuing problems at home, I was assigned a social worker. I don't know how this happened, but I'm guessing it was either the school or my mother who initiated it.

Her name was Irene. I was still dealing with bedwetting issues at this time. One week, I'd visit her in a comfortable room in a house funded by the local authority. We'd just talk about my day and how I felt.

I would listen to music of my choice. It felt nice that she cared enough to listen to me. There was even a star chart for tracking my progress, i.e. documenting how I felt. A star would be given and put on the chart if I didn't wet the bed.

The next few years of my life were filled with misery. The bullying and harassment continued, even after we moved three times within the same area. No matter which school I attended, it made no difference.

I was still chased and picked on, and for some reason, I seemed to stand out as vulnerable and easy to target. I felt invisible in a crowd, like I didn't belong anywhere or have anyone to connect with.

Everywhere I went, there was nothing positive to be found. I can still vividly recall the humiliation of that day in class. As I took my seat, a mischievous student slyly pushed my chair away from me, causing me to lose balance and fall unceremoniously to the floor.

The sound of laughter filled the room as I struggled to regain my composure. My cheeks burned with embarrassment as the instigator taunted me, ready for a fight with no apparent motive. It was a moment that would stick with me, a cruel reminder of how senseless bullying can be.

Chapter 10
Close Encounters

Over time, I started to make a few friends outside of school, which was quite remarkable. The friends I knew would hang out and chill at a grown-up's house called A. I guess it could be seen more like a 'youth club' environment.

I went along to a gathering at A's house; I did not suspect anything wrong. As I said, the hangout was seen as more like a 'youth club' to chill. I guess, being young, I was a bit naive. As it happened, I chose to wear a comfortable pair of shorts that day.

I remember them being Fred Perry, light blue shorts. Whilst I was just talking with different people, the atmosphere was filled with conversation. An unpleasant situation was about to occur and changed my feeling of safety forever.

Without my knowledge, the man named A, who ran the 'youth club', had touched my thigh whilst I was standing up and talking to others. I looked down and noticed his hand on me; I felt a sudden rush of shock.

I didn't know whether the contact was an accident or not, but it certainly left me feeling violated and uneasy. After this incident, I quickly left the property, filled with confusion and nervousness. I reported what had happened to my family. I vaguely remember a visit was made to the property to confront A. I am not sure what transpired after that.

That experience changed my understanding of personal space. It made me increasingly suspicious and afraid of being seen undressed or touched in an unwelcome way. Searching for a safe place, I began to only change clothes in private cubicles, far away from any prying eyes.

Even using a public toilet became a source of stress. I was paranoid about another person unintentionally looking at me. I opted to take refuge in a cubicle, regardless of how long I had to wait for it to become free.

I often find myself unable to open up even to close friends and family about these issues and cannot even bring myself to talk about sex or be emotionally vulnerable.

Eventually, I found out that A had been taking advantage of those in the 'youth club' setting. Grateful that I had managed to escape, I promised never to put myself in a similar situation again.

One day, sometime after it all happened, I spotted A walking outside around the local area. He was wearing dark sunglasses and a black jacket, and his hair was blonde. It seemed like he had left the area whilst under police surveillance and following public concerns.

In hindsight, I know that there were signs I missed at the time, but all I wanted was somewhere to be with other people. This experience taught me that you can never be too careful, and awareness is key to protecting yourself and keeping yourself safe.

Whilst living at home in my teens, I spent one particular night sleeping on the sofa in the front room. I am not sure what the reason was at the time, but I'm sure it was a valid one. P, my mother's boyfriend, was living with us at the time and had also invited his friend J, a painter and decorator who I think was homeless at the time, so he stayed with us for a short period.

Late one evening, whilst lying on the sofa, J started talking to me and for some reason, about his sexual orientation, which came up in conversation. He said something that made me feel very uncomfortable.

He offered to prove to me that he was gay if I didn't believe him, although I never said anything to disbelieve him, and why would I? I said nothing and pretended to have fallen asleep.

My fragmented memories of my teenage years remain murky, and I become conscious that I have subconsciously blocked out parts of them. In an attempt to understand what happened, I mentally construct a timeline of events, which helps me make sense of things.

An image of my younger self came to mind as I was writing this book. During my teenage years, I hung out with a girl around my age, and our group of friends were all using CB radios to chat with each other on the airwaves. That was the phase at the time.

The girl's mother would often join us in the conversations, and she seemed quite free and open with her behaviour. We'd hang out at her place and talk on the CB radio, or we would just chat about random things.

There are hazy memories of moments when I felt her touching my private parts whilst I was half asleep, but I pretended I was waking up, so she would move away from me quickly and hide what she was doing.

My mother must have sensed something suspicious because she soon took me away from that property. I guess, being young and curious and being a female, I did not see anything suspicious.

However, I knew it was not normal for a grown-up to act in such a way to a young person, but I didn't know what to do about it.

All these experiences left me feeling anxious and concerned, especially because I hadn't mentioned this to anyone until writing this book. As someone who has personally experienced these dangers, it is difficult to put into words the impact it has had on me.

The emotions that arise from such traumatic experiences are complex and overwhelming. Sharing my story is not easy, but if it helps raise awareness and protect others, then it is worth it.

The feelings that surfaced during and after those incidents are difficult to articulate. It was a mixture of fear, shame, and confusion. Trust, which is so essential, was shattered. These people manipulated my vulnerability, gradually eroding my boundaries and making me question my own worth.

Recognising the signs of this kind of abuse is critical for preventing further harm. It is essential to be vigilant and aware of changes in behaviour. The signs should never be dismissed or overlooked.

Trusting my instincts and being aware of these red flags might have spared me from experiencing such incidents. Staying safe requires a multifaceted approach. Education plays a crucial role in empowering young boys and girls to understand their rights, set boundaries, and recognise when they are being manipulated.

Open and honest communication is vital, allowing girls and boys to speak up about their experiences without fear of judgment or blame.

Building a support network is also essential. Surrounding oneself with trusted individuals who genuinely care and will listen without judgment has been instrumental.

It is important to remember that staying safe is not solely an individual responsibility. It is a collective effort. We must foster a society where we look out for one another, report suspicious behaviour and support others.

Chapter 11
Hopeful

I always had the feeling that I was different. I was always in my own little world, fascinated by how things worked, which, I guess, as I look back now, was my escapism. As a young kid, I would take things apart, such as stereos and televisions, bits from radios and all kinds of other electrical equipment.

I would put them back together again or even make something completely different with parts of the original product. I would then plug it in and see what happens. All too often, this resulted in blowing the fuse box, which would take out the power supply for the entire house. My mother would then angrily shout my name in frustration.

I remember being around 13 or 14 years old, and my mother bought me a Commodore 16+ computer for Christmas. I didn't go out; I had no friends, and I was a loner.

I found comfort and enjoyment in copying programs from the computer manual and seeing the finished program display itself on the screen. Back then, the goal was to understand the computer manual and what made up a computer program.

The idea of turning your creative vision into something I could experience was always appealing, but it wasn't as alluring as simply wanting to understand and ask an adult for help every step of the way and nurture the talent or interest I had.

I don't blame my mother, but I feel that any parent would want their child to explore further in what sparked their interest and develop it further.

At that time, without any outside help or push from parents, teachers, friends, or mentors, my enjoyment of computer programming and solo gaming sessions on the computer for hours did not progress into anything further for years until I was an adult.

I remember always having a dream of being in an influential boardroom in Canary Wharf and making powerful decisions. I didn't understand what it meant then, but the feeling stayed with me. I felt like there was something bigger for me than the life I was living.

I had to leave secondary school at 15 due to a situation at school that I had no control over and I was not involved in. However, I remember my mother pulling me out of school, insisting that the school had treated me like a criminal, though it broke my heart.

I could never understand what she thought she was protecting me from. I never registered with another school or continued studying at all. I do understand that any mother would want to protect her son, whatever the circumstances.

However, this led to me leaving school with no qualifications and therefore, unskilled labour was all that seemed to be available to me at the time. I had no GCSEs or qualifications sought.

However, my experiences have taught me that any job, no matter how menial, requires a certain skill set. To this day, the thought of leaving school early still aches in my chest, especially when I think about what could have been with the right support in place.

I fondly recall the limited options available to me as I searched for employment. My go-to sources were the back pages of the News Shopper and South London Press, where I scoured for warehouse jobs that could keep me afloat financially.

I eventually understood how holding on to what could have been, could be seen as restraining me from where I was now and my future potential. My experiences made it clear that aiming for the future was more important than reflecting on the past.

Once I adopted this attitude, I started to think about my future with a new determination. I unhanded the past's grasp over me, particularly concerning missed chances and directed my energy towards making objectives and planning ahead.

Instead of feeling bad about alternatives I didn't pick, I focused on building the life I wanted. Every step towards my goals motivated me more and brought me nearer to reaching them. The past certainly changed me, but it did not decide me.

It is the choices I made at the time and in the days that really counted. I think we can all get caught up in thinking why me or have the feelings of being 'stuck'.

The feeling of being trapped in the clutches of my past, suffocated by the weight of missed opportunities, by no fault of my own. It's as if I'm chained to a timeline that refuses to move forward, constantly reminding me of my failures.

The familiar feeling of being stuck engulfs me, leaving me yearning for a way out. But I do realise that I have the power to reflect, to dig deep within myself and confront the choices that have led me here.

I stand at the crossroads, my past on one side and my future on the other. I have a choice; to continue living the same life I've been living, defined by my past and tragedies, or to break free from those chains and create a new path for myself. I choose the latter.

I refuse to be defined by my past, to be the person who succumbs to its weight and limitations. I refuse to let it hold me back any longer. At this moment, I make a conscious decision to rewrite my story to mould a future that aligns with my aspirations and values.

It won't be easy, but the mere possibility of transformation fuels my determination. I gather the lessons of my experiences and life, using them as stepping stones towards a brighter tomorrow. I embrace the opportunity for growth and change, and I am ready to face whatever challenges may come my way.

As I take my first steps towards this new future, I feel a sense of freedom and empowerment wash over me. I am no longer confined by my past but instead driven by the hope and potential of what lies ahead. And as I walk towards my future, I leave behind the weight of my past, ready to embrace all that is to come.

Chapter 12
The Journey Begins

Life is full of surprises, and you never know what path is set out to follow. At 15 years old, I still lived with my mother; however, thanks to her 'encouragement' and pushing me outside of the house, I had made some friends in the area.

Being an introvert, it's challenging for me to connect with people. But having a shared passion for hip-hop music makes things easier. It's always surprising who you can meet after visiting a record shop and holding a hip-hop record under your arm. Sometimes, these conversations lead to unexpected connections when you least expect it.

At the age of 15, my interests led me down a creative path that would change my life forever. I discovered a passion for writing poems and raps. It was a form of expression that allowed me to pour my emotions and thoughts onto paper, giving me a voice that felt authentic and powerful.

During this transformative time, fate intervened, and I crossed paths with a like-minded individual who shared my love for music. I am still friends with them to this day. This chance encounter led to a long-standing friendship.

He became my DJ, and he would add beats from samples to my lyrics, creating a harmonious blend of words and music that resonated with us. I can still recall the moment I wrote my first rap during a physics lesson at school. That's where my enthusiasm for music and rap began.

Together, we delved into the world of rap, spending countless hours perfecting our performances. Our shared passion fuelled our determination, and we started performing at school community festivals in our area.

We found support in a local youth club that appreciated our talents and gave us resources to develop them. We had access to mentors and spaces where we could showcase our music and were surrounded by people who were just as passionate about it as we were.

Our dedication and hard work paid off, and our name began to gain recognition within our community. We were even featured in the *Mercury* newspaper, an exhilarating moment that validated our efforts and gave us a taste of wider acknowledgement.

We even had a radio interview. Throughout this journey, music became more than just a hobby; it became a lifeline, a means of self-discovery and empowerment. It taught us the power of collaboration, the importance of nurturing our creative passions, and the impact our art could have on others.

Looking back, those years of writing poems and raps and performing at community festivals taught me valuable lessons about teamwork and pursuing what I love. It was a time of self-expression, growth, and the realisation that with passion and support, anything is possible.

The memories of that transformative period still hold a special place in my heart, reminding me of the profound impact that art and community can have on shaping our lives.

Even though we didn't make it big or get signed, the journey was worth it.

My mother told me to get out of the house on a regular basis. I began spending time with other people who loved music as much as I did. Pretty soon, my friends and I started going to the West End, where we'd drink and hang out like any typical teenager.

It didn't take long before I got into cannabis and other illegal substances. Experiencing these new things was more important than worrying about the possible repercussions. Nonetheless, after many years of smoking cannabis, I eventually quit after it made me feel nauseous and paranoid instead of feeling good.

Whilst I was finding my social freedom, a friend of mine had a ticket to a disco event organised by McDonald's. He had got two tickets because he had known an employee. Initially, I wasn't too keen on the idea and had reservations about attending.

However, something inside me made me reconsider and little did I know that this decision would have a profound impact on my life. When I arrived, the disco lights flashed all over the place.

A woman caught my attention who was looking at me. She then approached me. Her confident demeanour and smile instantly drew me in. We engaged in conversation, and the connection between us was instant. I remember us both standing outside the disco.

She grabbed my pint of beer, poured it away without any explanation, and said, "You will not be needing that." I had no idea what this action meant in the long term.

I remember having to borrow a pair of trousers, a shirt, and shoes from my friend to attend the disco. It was a small act, but it made me feel more presentable, boosting my confidence and allowing me to feel like I belonged in that vibrant atmosphere.

Despite the borrowed outfit, I tried my best to exude self-assurance, hoping to convey that I was doing alright. Little did I know that this encounter, born out of a disco night and a borrowed ensemble, would mark the beginning of something different.

Those small moments when we overcome our fears and take risks can be the most life-changing ones. It was at that disco where I would meet my new girlfriend. Considering my childhood experiences and lack of friends, my life was starting to change.

Chapter 13
You Never Know

After meeting my new girlfriend at the disco arranged by McDonald's in 1988 at the age of 16, I recall meeting her at college almost a week later. We took a stroll through a park, and she plucked out a piece of paper from my wallet with contact numbers on it and stated, "You won't need this."

After getting to know each other for about a year or more, she moved in with me and my mother. Sadly, she was told to leave her previous accommodation, where she was staying with a family friend, who I believe did not approve of me.

We lived in the downstairs patio extension, looking out onto the back garden. My family were living upstairs. I kept it tidy and orderly, just as I always had when I was younger; my need for control, making sure everything in our space was neat, had never left me.

Though we were only dating, it was almost like we were living together as a couple already. My patio had also become a refuge for my friends if they ever got kicked out or needed help. My mum was kind enough to let them stay with us during these times of need. She was quite forgiving like that.

I remember getting a phone call from my girlfriend's older brother and 'giving me the talk'. At the time, I was employed as a warehouse assistant, and I did not really have any qualifications or direction in life.

I guess he was worried for his sister's future, which I could understand. I started working in various jobs from 16 years of age. I also moved out and got my own flat. I was offered a property after applying to the local council because I was still constantly having difficulties at home.

Unfortunately, it didn't end well; I was burgled shortly after. I also believe I was not mature or in the right frame of mind to look after a property at the time. I had moved back home for a very short period and returned my flat to the council.

My girlfriend had already moved into temporary housing by that time. I left home soon after and moved in with her. My girlfriend had then become pregnant.

It was not until August of 1990 that my daughter came into the world. This caused me to reflect on how I was going to support a family and consider my future options. In October of that same year, two of my girlfriend's colleagues became our witnesses as we got married at 18 years old.

I had no other clothing to wear except for jeans and a T-shirt, since my old flat had been burgled a few weeks prior and had taken everything, including my clothes and food. Right after the registry office ceremony was done, I rushed off to apply for a social fund loan from the Department of Health and Social Security.

Strangely enough, I did not inform anyone about us getting married. Looking back, I should have told people; that would have been the right thing to do. Years later, although I don't regret my decision, I wouldn't advise someone else to follow in my footsteps. It's important to think carefully before making any life-changing decisions at such a young age.

I recall that time I had called my mother to let her know that I had just gotten married. My sibling showed up later that day and berated me for it. Thinking about it now, I would have probably done the same thing due to the shock of the news.

My mother was displeased with the news of me getting married so young with a child on the way. What made it worse was that the marriage was on the same day as her birthday.

It was not until two years later, in 1992, that my son was born. I then chose to leave my warehouse job and filed paperwork with the Department of Health and Social Security to apply for the employment training government program.

Normally, those who seek employment benefits are required to wait six months before being accepted into the program. My case was special because of my circumstances and sheer determination to express in a letter that I wanted to change my career and future; now, I had children.

We both agreed to take classes further down the line. It was the plan of college that was our real goal; something stable, something secure for both of us and the children. We planned on attending a community college and then continuing onward. I was slowly starting to realise my achievements and ability through planning.

As parents, we were driven to create a better future for our children. However, without any guidance or mentorship, we were left to find our own path. We understood that education was key to improving our chances and achieving success in the future.

Chapter 14
Opportunities

I hadn't expected it to be easy. I left my warehouse job in 1993 and applied for a government-funded course. I requested less than the required six months to wait to start the course, half expecting to be turned down.

But to my surprise, I was accepted onto the Sight and Sound College course for a National Vocational Qualification in Business Administration Level 1-2, which took about a year to complete.

It was an encouraging start. It was the first course I would pass outside of school, and I felt a sense of pride as I received my certificate through the post. I wasted no time in heading down to the job centre holding my certificate in my hand, hoping to find some roles in administration to get me started.

Back then, it was looking at cards on a board with job details visible. There were no electronic boards or systems. I was frustrated with the lack of opportunities available to me from the job centre.

I sent a letter to the Prime Minister at the time, informing that there were no jobs available where I could start to cement a career path, as I wanted to improve my future.

To my surprise, after not too long, a response arrived from Number 10 to the job centre. I knew this because there was a buzz in the place when I arrived. The staff around me was in a frenzy; they were supporting me and questioning me on my ambitions, ideas, objectives, and prospects. I think they were taken aback at the initiative I had taken.

I secured a position as a Transport Coordinator, arranged by the job centre, after attending the 'Guaranteed Interview Scheme'. The position included organising and delivering components around the UK.

Unfortunately, I had to endure racist banter and behaviour from my colleagues, who assumed I wouldn't mind them saying offensive remarks about black people because I was white.

They even knew that my wife was black. Despite this annoyance, I stayed in the job since it provided my livelihood, and I had no choice but to stay. Unexpectedly, one day, life gave me an opportunity for something different.

My primary operation was managing transportation, but it seemed I wasn't so good at it. My manager assigned me to walk around different parts of the building, dispensing ticket numbers that correlated with the equipment reaching its destination.

Sometime later, I was called into the manager's office, only to be laid off after half a year of working. As depressing as it first sounded, it eventually worked in my favour without me having to make a move. It's incredible what can happen when you least expect it.

After being made redundant, I started to apply for other jobs. I remember looking at the *South London Press* and the

News Shopper, which were always my go-to favourites. I kept a list of job openings that I applied for during that time.

If memory serves, in one month, I had sent out almost sixty applications, ranging from entry-level to director positions, as I had kept the applications to visually see how many I had applied for.

I finally received an invitation from one of the applications I had completed. I was offered an interview for a clerical assistant post at the local council. My NVQ Level 1-2 qualification gave me an edge, and I was offered the job on a temporary basis.

Upon completion of my contract, I then searched again for a position in the council, which took approximately three months. I was then successful in applying for the role of benefits assistant in the housing benefits team.

I got a phone call after the interview telling me I had got the job. This was a permanent role, and I stayed in that position for the next six years. I felt that this was the pivotal point of my employment journey.

I remember buying our first fridge freezer with my first wages. With newfound confidence and the experience I had gained, I then successfully applied for a role as a benefits assessor in another local authority.

Growing up, I was never quite sure what it was that kept me going. I always wanted to push to make something of myself despite the odds, but looking back, when I was younger, I did not know how to do it.

I realise that it was resilience born from hard times that motivated me to strive for betterment and greater success. The thing about adversity is that it can ignite a spark in someone, urging them to make sure they never have to endure such difficulties again. It's this hunger for change and progress that keeps us moving forward, even when we think we are content.

After working as a benefits assessor for some time, I had already planned to move within the local authority. I was finally given a chance to shine. I then moved and applied for a job as a housing benefits verification officer in the same local authority.

This entailed checking IDs for housing benefit applications after a stint in that role for approximately two years, I applied to be an emergency duty officer with another local authority.

I recall the day I visited the offices for the interview. After a few days, I received a call with good news. I had been successful, and the job was mine. The moment of victory was exhilarating, as this role was like no other. I worked as an emergency duty officer for the next six years.

The role of the emergency duty officer was unique and unlike any of the previous positions I had taken before. Each day was a new experience with different conditions and requirements, which made the job thrilling and required a lot of responsibility.

In this position, I was placed at the forefront of emergency aid. My job was protecting people in need. I was not fully conscious of the magnitude of the role I had. I had to have a quick and accurate reaction in my position, and any errors could have lasting effects on a person's life.

Responding to emergency calls demanded clear-headedness and the capacity to rapidly reach a decision. Each request that came through had me collecting essential facts, evaluating the seriousness of the situation, and pinpointing the best course of action.

It was important to remain balanced and understanding whilst assuring the caller that aid was on route. Collaboration was an important part of this position. I collaborated closely with a group of devoted experts, including ambulance personnel, police, and firefighters.

Uncovering my unknown strengths is nothing less than incredible! It's like unlocking a hidden potential within myself, which fills me with power and excitement. The journey of self-discovery taught me that I am capable of doing things beyond my imagination. I discovered that being outside of my comfort zone in the roles that I have done leads to personal growth.

The unique experience I had gained inspired me to apply for the reviewing officer (social work assistant) position in the same local authority. I remember coming straight off a twelve-hour shift to attend the interview.

My determination never withered, as I would always think about where I had come from. I am happy to say I was successful in getting the job. During my time as a social work assistant, I had the honour of helping people in need.

My roles involved doing intake interviews, appraising their needs, and supplying them with resources and aid. In conjunction with social workers, I constructed care plans and connected clients with community services.

Additionally, I ran support groups, managed workshops, and promoted my client's rights and welfare. Each day presented new challenges and chances to change someone's life in a positive way; it was immensely rewarding to be part of their quest for healing and empowerment.

At the start of my journey, I held onto an inherent sense that something big was coming; although what it was, I had no idea. The steps ahead of me felt like leaps of faith, guided by a never-ending curiosity and a strong faith in my dreams. Though they appeared small, these steps could reveal unexpected potential.

As I embarked on this journey towards something big, I found myself on a path paved with unknown possibilities. Each step I took and am still taking, feels like a leap of faith, guided by an insatiable curiosity and an unwavering belief in the power of dreams.

The stepping stones before me, though seemingly small, hold the potential to unlock extraordinary opportunities. With each milestone I encounter, I am reminded that the destination remains shrouded in mystery.

Yet, I am unyielding in my determination to forge ahead, embracing the uncertainty that accompanies this pursuit. I understand that true beauty lies not just in the final destination but in the transformative power of the journey itself.

The paths set out before me, seemingly ordinary at first glance, reveal themselves to be catalysts for growth and self-discovery.

As I traverse them, I learn valuable lessons, gather new insights, and acquire skills that equip me for the challenges that lie ahead. They push me outside my comfort zone, forcing me to confront my fears and embrace the unknown.

I certainly delved into the unknown when a chance arose to apply for a sponsorship to undertake a social work degree with the local authority. In order to be successful, I had to make it through an interview with the local authority, an IT assessment, and a written test from the university to be considered for the course.

The day of the interview arrived; I could feel the weight of its significance pressing upon me. This was not just any interview; it felt like the interview of my life. My chances of achieving my ambition of becoming a social worker were dependent on how I did in the tests and interviews.

The next challenge I faced was the IT test with the local authority. I nervously took my seat and stared at the computer screen with anticipation. The test questions were designed to evaluate my technical knowledge and how well I could solve problems.

Each movement of the mouse brought me closer to my desired future, spurring me to do my best. I concentrated hard and drew upon all my preparation, knowing this was a vital obstacle in my path. My interest in IT played a part that day.

In the next step, I grabbed a pen and began to answer the university's written test. My answers had to be thoughtful, demonstrating my academic knowledge as well as my enthusiasm for social work and my passion for articulating my thoughts.

It was daunting, but I used that pressure to help me concentrate on expressing my dedication wholeheartedly. Reflecting on my past, I recalled what had led me here and where I hoped to go in the future.

Throughout the entire process, the sheer determination to be selected for the social work degree overwhelmed me. This was my calling, my purpose, and I was willing to give everything I had to make it a reality.

Every question, every written word, carried the weight of my aspirations and the countless hours of preparation that had led me to this point. The thought of not being selected was unbearable.

It was a thought I pushed aside, refusing to entertain the possibility of falling short. I knew deep down that this was the path I was meant to pursue, and I was willing to fight for it with every ounce of my being.

The outcome was uncertain, but I knew that I had given it my all. The journey to reach this point, from where I had come from, had been filled with sacrifices and unwavering determination.

Now, it was in the hands of fate. I could only hope that my efforts would be recognised months later; when I received the news of my acceptance into the social work degree program, a wave of relief and joy washed over me.

The weight that had been resting on my shoulders was lifted, replaced by a sense of accomplishment and gratitude. The interview of my life had proved successful, and I was ready to embark on the next chapter of my journey towards becoming a social work professional.

I am happy to say that it took three years, but I qualified as a social worker with a 2:1 BA (Hons) degree in 2012. I am the first person in my family ever to go to university. It took quite a few steps, and I am still on my journey.

My work in the field of social work provided me with a valuable perspective on the challenges I faced as a youth. Whilst my clients had grown into adults, their underlying struggles remained.

It was enlightening to recognise that these issues can impact individuals of any age. After four years as a social worker, I progressed to senior social worker and eventually became a team manager.

My experiences in social work inspired me to pursue higher education, leading me to become a qualified Best

Interest Assessor (BIA) and undertake independent assessments. In my role of safeguarding vulnerable adults and advocating for their well-being, I found solace in being able to protect those who may not have had someone to protect them in their younger years.

It is true that life constantly keeps us on our toes. Just when we think everything is as it should be, something out of the blue throws our plans out of whack. Such sudden changes can be disorienting and often leave us feeling overwhelmed.

When life surprises me with a curveball, it's almost as if the ground beneath me suddenly shifts, whether this be new opportunities or events.

Chapter 15
What Is Success

At the beginning of the book, I mentioned how I always dreamed of being in a powerful boardroom in Canary Wharf, making influential decisions. However, it didn't quite turn out that way.

My drive for success, in any form, was still strong within me. Throughout the years, I developed a passion for computers and became skilled at maintaining them. Soon enough, I was fixing other people's computers as well.

I even started selling them, but customers would often demand updates and additional equipment after their purchase. Dealing with these confrontations or 'difficult' situations made me uncomfortable and managing conversations felt challenging, even in my 20s.

Over the years, I had pursued numerous ventures in my efforts to reach the metaphorical boardroom. From creating websites for IT training to designing products that never made it off paper, I was constantly moving on to my next idea.

Lack of support and opportunities hindered me from turning these ideas into reality. I even tried crowdfunding, only to be met with disappointment and no funding. It made me think about all the other individuals like me, striving to bring their ideas to fruition and make a positive impact on their lives and the lives of others.

I recall my days of selling electronic goods at a flea market, then moving on to providing computers and delivering them. I used to go around distributing leaflets, informing people about the computer training services I offered.

But as hard as I tried, nothing came back. I would often sit down and think about; what can I do that is really going to change my life and the lives of others. It was almost like an obsession of wanting to just keep moving forward, in whatever form that meant.

It was not until around 2010, I thought of an idea called 'Immortal Stories'. This is where stories never end, and it is for the reader to contribute to the first chapter's scenario of events and then it is further updated by other users. However, only imagination is allowed.

Like other things, this just remains on the internet, as a testament of my pursuit of dreams and a reminder of what can be achieved. Even though the idea did not 'take off', this was a success for me.

I had never been in any position to even contemplate starting anything when I was young, and here I was being able to spread my wings, without judgement or being curtailed.

As I continued to navigate through life, trying out different ventures and ideas, I realised that success was not just about achieving big goals or reaching the metaphorical boardroom.

It was also about the small victories and moments that shaped my journey. These moments were often overlooked but were significant, nonetheless.

I started to shift my definition of success from external achievements to personal growth and fulfilment. Instead of constantly chasing after 'the next big thing', I began focusing on how I could positively impact those around me with whatever resources or skills I had at that moment.

Although I had adopted a positive mind-set, there were still moments where self-doubt and frustration consumed me. As someone trying to break into the world of entrepreneurship with limited resources and no connections, it often felt like there were constant barriers blocking my progress.

But rather than giving up, these challenges only strengthened my determination to find alternative paths towards achieving my goals. We all encounter individuals who leave a lasting impact on us throughout our lives, and for me, that person was David Boice.

He encouraged me to not only embrace successes but also learn from failures and develop strategies to overcome them. The conversations I had were inspirational and he made me think of my future and what I wanted out of it.

One phrase he said that has stuck with me forever is 'punch above your weight', which has helped me recognise my own potential and strive for greatness. A line that I often say to the people I meet, wanting to excel into their next job role.

As well as being a social worker, David is a life coach. I was very fortunate to have the company of this great asset all to myself during my lunch break. The conversations enlightened me, before having to return to the duty desk.

I often remind myself that success can take on various forms, and it's important to recognise and value each one. As

I sit here in the present moment, I contemplate how I can make a positive impact on the world.

Ultimately, whether or not my efforts have made an impact will be determined by others long after I am gone.

Chapter 16
Determination

Speaking from my own life experiences and from the perspective of being a young father, having two children at the young age of 19 was an incredibly overwhelming experience.

The struggles I faced, both financially and emotionally, have shaped me in ways I never could have anticipated and in a positive way. One of the most immediate challenges I encountered was the financial strain.

Suddenly, I found myself responsible not only for my own needs, which I could barely meet but also for the needs of others. The weight of providing for a family with two children and ensuring their well-being became a constant source of worry.

Balancing the demands of work, planning, education, and the future whilst finding affordable childcare and meeting the basic necessities became an ongoing juggling act. The constant pressure about money and the fear of not being able to meet the children's needs created a significant concern that weighed heavily on me.

Lacking qualifications impacted my ability to earn a sustainable income. I quickly realised the urgency of bringing in income to support my family. With a deep sense of responsibility, I took on various jobs to make ends meet, doing whatever it took to ensure the rent was paid and there was food on the table.

My career path at that time was diverse, ranging from warehouse labour to restaurant positions like McDonald's and KFC. I worked hard to juggle multiple jobs at once in order to make the most of my income.

Performing laborious tasks in a warehouse whilst working in the fast-paced environment of the food industry was difficult, yet the goal of providing for my children kept me motivated. You eventually understand that you must do what you must to get by, and no job is beneath you.

I didn't limit myself to a single job; I accepted positions from temporary agencies so that I could gain different experiences. From fur factories to food packaging, carpeting to envelop stuffing and roofing to sweeping, it was a chance to learn a variety of skills.

Regardless of the task, packing boxes, assembling products, or helping with administrative duties, I was up for the challenge. Although the work was often taxing and boring, this allowed me to create an income for my family.

Despite the challenges, I learnt valuable lessons during those years. I developed a strong work ethic, resilience in the face of hardship, and a resourceful mind-set. I honed my time management and organisational skills as balancing work and family became a delicate balancing act.

Moreover, I gained a deep appreciation for the value of every pound earned and learnt to budget wisely to ensure our basic needs were met.

Whilst the jobs I held during that time may not have aligned with my long-term aspirations, they served as steps towards a brighter future. I knew that gaining qualifications and acquiring new skills were essential for upward mobility.

As my children grew older, I worked towards obtaining an education and sought opportunities for career advancement. This was a joint decision between me and my wife for the betterment of the family.

Reflecting on the past, I feel a surge of pride for the sacrifices my family and I made. The relentless determination I displayed to provide for my loved ones fills me with a sense of accomplishment.

Through the trials and challenges of those years, I learnt to tap into my inner strength and channel it towards creating a better life. Those experiences instilled in me a deep-seated resilience and an unwavering drive to never give up.

Being a young parent can be overwhelming. I had to grow up quickly and make decisions that would impact not only my own life but also the life of my family. The transition from adolescence to parenthood was abrupt.

I often felt a sense of loss for the carefree years. There were times when I questioned my abilities as a parent and wondered if I was equipped to handle the immense responsibility that came with it.

The judgment and criticism from others who questioned having children at such a young age added to the emotional strain.

It seemed I was thrust into the challenges of parenthood without a support network or guidance from someone with more life experience. It was lonely to navigate through parenting whilst trying to find like-minded individuals who could offer a helping hand.

To make things worse, many of my friends were busy with other priorities in their lives and couldn't relate to my situation. The emotional and psychological weight of feeling isolated and misunderstood compounded upon me.

When picking up my kids from school, I'd wait alone at the playground and observe all the older parents conversing amongst themselves. Rather than try to approach them, I kept to myself and just waited for my children instead.

My wife looks back with joyous memories of our early years, which I can understand, and I can remember aspects to some degree. I wish I could have and remember the same memories.

However, that time sadly was filled with immense pressure, owing money that seemed impossible to repay and striving to keep my family from further debt. Even though things were tough, I have always loved my children and would not have had it any other way.

I always pushed for the need to stay afloat. This was the only out, and I wished for everyone's well-being to survive. Now, these same children who I mentioned at the time of writing this book are 31 and 33.

They have become thoughtful and considerate people who are making their mark in the world. They have both discovered careers as musicians, producers, and models. They never sit still but instead find excitement in experiencing new things and facing challenges head-on.

As my children grew into adults, I thought that our relationship would have become easier and more fulfilling, but I quickly realised that this was not the case. Despite my love for them, I struggle to express my feelings towards them in a way that they could understand.

My difficulty in communicating my emotions and thoughts often leads to misunderstandings and conflicts. I have always been a reserved person, keeping my feelings and thoughts to myself.

This has caused a lot of frustration for those closest to me, especially my children. They have expressed feeling disconnected from me because of my lack of physical affection and communication.

I never grew up in an environment where showing physical affection or expressing emotions was a common practice. This is also something that does not come naturally to me. I struggle with initiating hugs or saying, 'I love you', even though I try to feel it deeply inside.

The same goes for phone calls or other forms of communication. Whilst some people find comfort in talking on the phone, I have always felt uncomfortable with it. This lack of communication has undoubtedly created a rift, as they may interpret it as me not caring enough about their lives.

This couldn't be further from the truth. In fact, I am constantly thinking about them and worrying about their well-being. But despite all these challenges, we have still managed to build a strong relationship based on mutual respect and understanding.

We may not communicate in traditional ways, but we have found our own way of connecting with each other. One thing that has helped is our shared love for music. As mentioned before, both my children have pursued careers in music, and we can bond over our passion for it.

We have attended concerts together and shared playlists with each other. I also try to show my love through actions rather than words or physical affection.

However, I hope they understand that even if the words aren't there, I am always thinking of them. When and if they read this book, maybe they will gain more insight into who I am and the journey I have had to take.

Chapter 17
The Year 2019–2020

My life took a very different turn in 2019. A colleague named AJ, whom I had met six years earlier, was a mentor for me at the time I had applied for a government business start-up loan. I was in Morrison's car park after shopping.

AJ had called me to ask if I was interested in an opportunity to work for a newly formed Care Recruitment Agency as a registered manager. He had previously supported me whilst I was trying to develop an idea for an app for social services, which did not take off, and we remained contacts on LinkedIn.

I was told that the position would involve working with staff, carers, and local authorities, as well as private clients. I would also provide training and supervision. I was the fifth person to be interviewed for the position. I questioned whether this was fate or was it meant to be.

The prospect of being interviewed by the Care Quality Commission to become a registered manager instilled in me both excitement and apprehension. This monumental next step in my career had me eager to demonstrate my knowledge and commitment to delivering excellent care.

There was no doubt that my duties as an emergency duty officer, combined with my experience in social work, had served me well. I am proud to say that in 2019, I obtained my registered manager status, and I continued to keep up my social work registration as well.

I started this position part-time to concentrate on my social work duties. Things were going very well, but then the pandemic struck, and it slowed down considerably around March 2020.

Almost everyone in every industry was affected by the pandemic. We were trying to drum up business by looking for clients and tendering for a contract with the local authority.

The owners of the business were husband and wife, P and AJ. One September morning, AJ and his wife arrived at the office at about 9 am, and I got there at 8:30 am. Over time, it became apparent that AJ was more than just a colleague to me.

He was like a brother from another mother because we got on so well. I remember we would go for a walk and talk about life every afternoon. He religiously brought me a banana every day.

I also got on well with his wife, who was very nice, pleasant, and considerate, who saw the best in people and wanted them to excel. As I said, AJ arrived at 9 am with his wife on Tuesday.

He sat down opposite me and was smiling. We were talking about a visit that was done for a potential client the Friday before. His head suddenly jolted sharply up and then down, like he had been electrocuted. He then fell back slowly with an agonised expression across his face.

Initially, I thought his reaction was due to his sense of humour because he would always joke around. But it soon became apparent that something serious had happened. He quickly lost consciousness, and his wife began to scream whilst she was pacing in the office in a state of shock.

Instinctively, I called 999 and followed their instructions whilst undertaking CPR for about twenty minutes until the ambulance arrived and took over. Soon enough, after being assessed by the ambulance crew and an on-site doctor, AJ was declared dead in the office.

When AJ's body was taken away by the coroner, his wife was left in stunned silence. I could only imagine her silent grief and shock as she watched them wheel him away in a body bag.

As we left the office, an overwhelming sense of dread crept up my spine at the thought of the unthinkable tragedy that had just occurred. It was really strange because we both said goodbye outside the office, as we had done every day, but this was certainly different.

This time, AJ was taken by the coroner, and we both made our separate way home. I had phoned my wife and said, "AJ is dead." On the way home on the train, anxiety gnawed at me; I had a deep fear that what happened to AJ could at any time happen to me.

Every time I felt a small pain, I'd worry that it was a sign of some impending doom. This carried on for about six months. I wanted to run away from this trauma, but something inside urged me forward and compelled me to want to care for his family and his wife. So, every day, I called his wife to make sure she was okay and checked on the children.

Although I never told AJ's wife how it affected me, she said that she believed AJ put me there to care for and look after her because he knew he was going to die. This was a sentiment that other people had also voiced after hearing this story, even my wife.

I believe this because the sequence of events was that AJ had come out of his house with his wife, walked to the office building, got in the lift, walked along the corridor and into the office.

It was there he sadly passed away. I often think of the circumstances in which he came all that way, only to pass away in the office with myself and his wife present.

The bond that I have forged with AJ's widow through grief in the presence of death is a testament to the resilience of humankind and the power of a shared experience, albeit a very sad one.

From my own perspective, I have witnessed and experienced the profound impact that this bond can have on one's journey. The effects of witnessing a death in such a poignant context will forever be a part of me.

The loss may never fully fade, but through this journey, I have discovered it is important to hold onto the memories and the lessons learnt from the person who left us too soon. Their presence will always be a guiding light. It reminds me to cherish the precious moments we have with our loved ones and friends and to find strength.

It was only until after AJ's death I discovered that he used to live across the street from me with his brothers, sister and mother. I decided to visit the house that he had lived in when he was younger, which was owned by his wife.

Surprisingly, when standing on the balcony of his old home, I could see my mother's house right across the road. The sight of it left me astonished. I believe that the whole occurrence in the universe is a complex combination of different components, including natural laws, causality, and randomness.

Events are often guided by an amalgamation of circumstances, making each outcome unique. Although we may not always know or predict these events, they make up an intricate tapestry that contributes to the universe's existence.

Chapter 18
The Aftermath

It had been quite some time since the devastating loss of AJ, but we were determined to honour him by continuing with his vision for the company. Despite our best efforts, our progress was quickly halted because of the pandemic.

After much deliberation, we decided to move offices to save costs and seek out new clients, which was very difficult. It was then that AJ's wife mentioned how she wanted to go into the field of audiology.

It was an interesting transition since we were both in the social care and medical field. AJ's wife is a medic, so I was in good hands, and we progressed forward with the plan.

We arranged for builders to transform a room in the house into a clinic, and the job took about two months to finish. After it was completed, we acquired all of the necessary equipment and began to spread the word about the new facility.

We hired an audiologist, only for it not to work out as planned. We learnt that rather than relying on others, we decided to explore a completely new area by ourselves. Coupled with our experience, we enrolled in a course for micro-suction ear wax removal at Aston University in Birmingham.

Going on this journey brought both excitement and nervousness, but I was ready to help those who sought my assistance to get rid of their ear discomfort and improve their hearing.

During the training, I devoted myself to the study of audiology, ear anatomy, and the processes involved in safe and effective ear wax removal. I was very interested in learning all about the inner workings of the ear and how much an accumulation of wax could affect someone's hearing and overall health. It reminded me of my own experience of having a hearing impairment. It felt like I had come full circle.

With the assistance of professionals and observations during the training, I picked up on the various techniques for ear wax removal, such as micro-suction and instrumentation. I sharpened my abilities through practical exercises and watched specialists carry out their work, gaining knowledge of the best approaches for client comfort and protection.

So, not only did I continue social work, but I also performed micro-suction. One could say the route is already planned or that life will take you where you need to go. I believe both of these views are true. So, you never know where life is going to take you.

In January 2023, I then embarked on a transformative journey and took the next step by enrolling in a course at South Devon University, with the support of the company and the experience of the micro-suction course.

The course was to qualify as a Hearing Aid Dispenser (HAD). I had also set my goal to complete a degree to become a qualified audiologist after completing the HAD course. This decision marked a significant shift in my career path as I ventured further into the field of audiology.

A completely different area from my previous endeavours. My interview was with Antonio Specchia (Giulio), and little did I know that this amazing lecturer would be pivotal in my educational journey.

The application process itself was a challenging endeavour, requiring me to showcase my passion for audiology, my willingness to learn, and my dedication to providing quality care and support to individuals with hearing impairments.

I underwent an interview demonstrating my commitment to the profession and my eagerness to make a positive impact on the lives of others. Upon receiving the news of my acceptance into the course, I felt a mixture of excitement and apprehension.

The realisation that I would be embarking on a comprehensive educational journey in hearing aid dispensing both thrilled and humbled me. I knew that the path ahead would be demanding, but I was ready to embrace the challenges and opportunities that awaited me.

I am overwhelmed by my success, though I know all too well the feeling of being held back. The people, whether this be family, friends, or colleagues, have been a part of my educational journey, including those who had noticed me, not only me but my ability to challenge myself and the belief that I will succeed.

It did seem like where I was from and my past was restricting me when I was younger. It was easy to think that nothing would ever come from me because of these roadblocks.

Then I began to realise that what was in front of me wasn't the entire picture, and those who are a part of my life showed me this. Though my history and experiences affected my starting line, they didn't decide how far I'd go.

I started the course in January 2023 and shared my learning disability of autism, which had been diagnosed in October 2023 and dyslexia in 2009.

The diagnosis of autism did not surprise me, as I had always thought I was different, but I could not understand why I displayed a particular behaviour or had difficulties in understanding and collective thoughts.

This was to ensure that arrangements and support were made for me. I was passing assignments, although it was very difficult. At the end of year one, in August 2023, I took a practical hearing test, and during this time, the test felt like my knowledge was being siphoned off from me.

Though the answers were right there in my head, they seemed unreachable. This prevented me from passing on two attempts for the final year practical exam. Being held back due to my learning difficulties was an incredibly difficult experience outside of my control.

I was determined to go at it again for a third time, with better strategies and resources in place to help. This included reassurance from Antonio Specchia (Giulio) and the positive feedback and outlook on everything.

I am happy to say that my third attempt at the practical assessment was a success, and I progressed to Level 5 of my course. It was a huge relief and showed me that my hard work had paid off. I am now in the process of completing Level 5, learning all about audiology and hearing aid technology.

I am so grateful for the incredible support system that has been put in place for me during my journey. My lecturers have been incredibly understanding and patient with me by allowing me extra time to complete tasks and offering feedback whenever needed.

Despite many challenges along the way, I am determined to make a positive impact on those living with hearing impairments, no matter where they are from or what their past may be like.

The path ahead is still long, but I look forward to continuing my journey into audiology and making my mark on this field. It's ironic that I have a hearing impairment, as it feels like I've come full circle to practice the very thing that I experienced.

I often feel like I'm constantly having to prove something to myself, always striving for improvement and growth. It's a way of moving forward from my past self and towards who I am now.

Funny enough, each opportunity I've taken and every course I've completed has pushed me further away from where I was before. And whilst I have no desire to go back to that place, I am grateful for the lessons it has taught me.

The qualities of determination, risk-taking, focus, and self-control are what continue to lead me on a successful path. The past has made me what I am in the present, and I welcome that.

Chapter 19
Adversity

Life has thrown countless adversities my way, testing my resilience and resolve. The moments of heartbreak, setbacks, and self-doubt that threatened to derail me. But with every setback, I found the strength to rise again.

No matter what it was, I managed to find a way to keep going instead of letting it define me. Despite my difficult past, I chose to look ahead and not see myself as a victim.

I have a hearing impairment. It's a part of who I am, and it has shaped my life's journey in ways I never could have imagined. Whilst it presents challenges, it has also strengthened my character as an adult and opened doors to experiences I wouldn't trade for anything.

Having a hearing impairment at a young age was a turning point in my life. It meant that my world was different from those around me, and communication became a unique puzzle to solve.

But I never let it define me or hold me back. Instead, growing up and now as an adult, I continue to have the opportunity to learn and adapt.

Life has thrown many challenges my way, as I also had to contend with dyslexia and autism. Like my hearing impairment, I never let them define me or hold me back, instead finding ways to use them to my advantage.

With routine and structure, everyday tasks become possible and manageable. However, it can be difficult for some to understand why the same routine is so important. It helps me manage my emotions and keeps me on track.

My resilience has been tested and stretched over the years, especially when it comes to dealing with emotions. There have been moments of crippling fear or severe anxiety that can take over, no matter how hard I try to control them.

But rather than letting these moments define me as a person, I use each experience as an opportunity to learn more about myself and who I am as a person.

At times, I have learnt that being on the autistic spectrum can make it extremely difficult for me to communicate my feelings and ideas. My mind is full of thoughts and emotions, but when I go to say them aloud, they come out jumbled, halting, or incomplete.

It's not because of a lack of intelligence or imagination; rather, my words just don't seem to follow the path I've mapped out in my head. It's like being stuck inside myself as I try desperately to get others to grasp what I'm conveying.

Despite the challenge, I am determined to find alternate ways of expressing myself through writing, art, and other forms that let me show who I am without inhibition.

It's hard for me to interact with people, particularly my adult children and other important people in my life, because of the difficulties I face with disabilities. Expressing my thoughts and feelings has always been a challenge, which is amplified when talking to those closest to me.

As a result of this communication barrier, misunderstandings and frustrations arise, leaving me feeling alone and unheard. It saddens me that I cannot express my love and worries or even have a basic conversation properly.

I fear that my family and others think that I am not interested or disconnected when really it is the issues that make it challenging for me to express my emotions.

I long for open conversations with my loved ones, but I feel that I am frequently held back by the fear of being misjudged. I'm searching for ways to bridge this gap between how I feel and what I can vocalise.

Although these issues persist, I remain intent on finding measures, such as patience and understanding from others that will permit me to move past these hindrances.

I cling to routines and orderliness. I organise my clothes in advance and keep my keys in the same spot each day in order to minimise confusion. Dyslexia impacts how I read, write, and comprehend language, making even basic tasks difficult.

Because of this, it can be exhausting trying to understand words and their meanings, which often leads to feelings of loneliness and isolation from people who don't understand.

My need to control goes beyond the external and infiltrates my internal world. I attempt to manage my thoughts, emotions, and actions in order to confront the difficulties which come with autism and dyslexia.

This striving for control has become a way to function in a world that often seems too much and too random. However, my craving for control can also be detrimental. It may provide a sense of steadiness and orderliness, but it might also hinder me from completely freeing myself and accepting spontaneity.

Being scared of being judged and messing up can block me from taking chances and discovering different paths. It's like I'm constantly balancing on a tightrope, trying to establish an equilibrium between authority and the capability to live in truthfulness.

With all that in mind, I would have never dreamed of having the positions that I have had, let alone gaining a degree or even moving into the field of audiology. We all possess the power and capacity to alter our circumstances, no matter who we are or where we come from.

When I look back on my past, it's not with any negative feelings but with a sense of pride and accomplishment, whatever our circumstances, disabilities, or abilities.

I believe everyone deserves equal access to communication and opportunities, regardless of their abilities. I've encountered misconceptions and stereotypes along the way. Some people assume that my hearing impairment and abilities limit my abilities or intelligence, but I've proved them wrong time and time again.

By having support and mechanisms in place, I've excelled academically and pursued my passions with unwavering determination. My abilities have not hindered my potential; if anything, they have fuelled my drive to prove that I can achieve anything I set my mind to.

I choose not to be defined by labels because, like everyone else in this world, we are all capable of greatness in our own unique ways. My hearing impairment, dyslexia and autism make up part of who I am today. I know that despite these conditions, I can still achieve what I want in life if only I stay strong until the end.

So, as I continue on my journey, I embrace all that is me. It has made me stronger, more compassionate, and more determined to make a difference in the lives of others. I am proud to be an advocate, a learner, and a beacon of inspiration for those who share my journey.

Chapter 20
Legacy and Beyond

As I conclude my memoir, I reflect on the legacy I want to leave behind. I'm driven to inspire others facing similar challenges and to offer a guiding light in their darkest moments.

My journey is not just about me; it's about the countless others who have faced growing up in dysfunctional, bullying, and violent and abusive backgrounds. I hope that by sharing my story, I can ignite a spark of hope, reminding others that they, too, can overcome their circumstances and forge their own path to success.

It took years for me to gain the confidence to step up and change my life. I always felt that I could rise above the chaos and brokenness of my upbringing, but it was daunting.

As a young person, I had an innate sense that I could take control of my life but didn't quite know how. But I knew deep down that if I wanted something different for myself, I had to be willing to make difficult decisions and take risks.

I found strength in the things that made me unique; the activities and people who made me feel alive and appreciated. Keeping a positive focus on these things gave me the courage to make big changes in my life, changes that eventually led me away from home and into a much more stable living situation. It wasn't without its challenges, but it was the right choice in order to live a normal and healthy life.

We all have something inside us, even if we don't know it at the time. This could be a desire for change and, most significantly, not allowing ourselves to be victims of our childhood experiences or environment.

It is not easy, but with hard work, determination, and self-belief, we can all create a future of possibility for ourselves, no matter what our pasts may look like. That is what has enabled me to move forward with strength and courage into the unknown without fear of failure or failure as an option.

I can't forget Rocky Balboa, the fictional character who became a role model for me. Such an unlikely hero, Rocky was an unlikely source of inspiration, yet he spoke to my inner yearnings and pushed me to overcome the odds stacked against me.

No matter how hard things got, I always found solace in Rocky's story, his unwavering belief in himself, his refusal to back down and his relentless pursuit of his dreams. His determination was infectious; it made me want to emulate him and succeed despite any obstacle life threw at me.

Whenever I felt overwhelmed by life, I turned to Rocky for guidance, drawing strength from a fictional world that began to feel more real than my own chaotic environment.

In times of distress, I would play 'Going the Distance' on repeat, watching Rocky fight until the very end and never giving up; it was as if he knew what I was going through and was rooting for me every step of the way.

As an adult today, I still think about Rocky whenever I'm navigating a difficult situation or feeling overwhelmed. His story helps me remember that no matter how insurmountable something might seem at first, it can be conquered with enough grit and courage.

Most importantly, though, Rocky reminded me that it's okay to dream big and, more importantly, take action on those dreams!

His iconic training montages became my motivation to push myself harder and never surrender to the circumstances that tried to hold me back. Rocky taught me the importance of resilience, discipline, and self-belief.

He showed me that even in the absence of a father, I could find strength within myself and rise above the obstacles that threatened to define me.

Whilst the pain of growing up without a father and enduring dysfunctional relationships has left its scars, Rocky Balboa's influence has been transformative. He taught me that heroes can come from unexpected places, even from the silver screen.

Through Rocky's example, I learnt to believe in myself, to fight for my dreams, and to never let my circumstances define my worth.

In my journey, Rocky Balboa became more than just a character; he became a symbol of hope, resilience, and power. As I continue to navigate through life's challenges, I carry his lessons in my heart, reminding myself that even without a father (to go forward), I can forge my own path and become the hero of my own story.

My journey does not end there; I am determined to pursue a master's degree and become a qualified audiologist. I believe our own actions determine the outcome of our story, but it is the people we encounter along the way who help us write it. Ultimately, we are the ones in control of the pen that shapes our narrative.

My thoughts are to never restrict oneself within the confines of the mind. Fear, like a heavy anchor, has the power to halt a person's progress and hinder them from reaching their true potential.

It is a daunting force that can paralyse even the bravest of souls and hold them back from greatness. Fear should not be able to control or limit actions. Embrace the unknown and push past fear to unlock the full capabilities of oneself. Only then will one truly achieve all that they are capable of.

Chapter 21
Dreams

Our dreams and desires hold little weight unless we actively put in the effort to make them a reality. I have spent countless hours developing ideas on paper. These stem from the idea of creating a social care app to creating and designing a role-playing game based purely on imagination.

However, without support and confidence from others, these ideas lay dormant because it is always challenging to move forward without support in place. Our determination can push us, but external factors such as our circumstances and access to resources can also play a significant role in our ability to achieve success.

Ultimately, it all comes back to us and the idea of being recognised for our endeavours; the question is, how do we reach that point?

We all have the ability to achieve greatness and make a positive impact in the world. However, sometimes we face barriers that hold us back from fully realising our potential. These barriers can come in various forms and can be caused by external circumstances or internal doubts and fears.

Lack of support and limited access to resources can hinder our progress towards our goals. Growing up in a low-income household, I often felt limited in my aspirations because I saw the struggles my family faced every day.

Getting a higher education seemed like an impossible dream, as we barely had enough money. The idea of starting my own business or pursuing a creative career felt out of reach due to financial constraints.

Furthermore, not having a strong support system can also be a barrier to achieving success. Without encouragement and guidance from those around us, it is easy to doubt ourselves and lose motivation towards our goals.

We all need someone who believes in us and pushes us to keep going when we feel like giving up. Moreover, access to resources such as education, technology, and opportunities plays a crucial role in our ability to reach our full potential.

Unfortunately, not everyone has equal access to these resources, which can create disparities in opportunities for success.

However, even if external barriers are removed or minimised, we still face internal barriers that hold us back from reaching our full potential. Fear of failure and self-doubt are common obstacles that prevent us from taking risks and pursuing our dreams wholeheartedly. It takes courage and resilience to overcome these internal barriers and step out of our comfort zone.

Despite these challenges, I believe that anyone has the ability to break through these barriers with determination and perseverance.

We must never let external circumstances or internal doubts define our capabilities or limit what we can achieve. Furthermore, society plays a significant role in breaking down these barriers. We must create a culture that embraces diversity and inclusivity, where everyone is equal.

Chapter 22
Notice Me

Before I began writing this book, I crafted a poem. A tribute to my passion for hip-hop and poetry. I see this as the catalyst for my memoir, which is a message to all of us craving recognition and validation.

We just want to be seen and noticed, and acknowledged for who we are. But I realise now that my story is not just about me; it is a tribute to those who shaped me, to my mentors, my friends, my family, even my enemies and to every person who believed in me and helped me to become the person I am today.

This final chapter is not just my story but a poem to all of us who strive to make our mark in a world that often overlooks us. This is our chance to be heard, our chance to be seen and acknowledged, and our chance to make a difference and to be remembered.

I hope my story inspires others to chase their dreams and never give up, for we are all worth noticing and being seen.

Notice Me
A Poem by R.B. Hill

I was born in Lewisham Hospital and lived in Heather Green Lane; the beginning of my life started with pain.

I was born with an illness straight from birth; my mother feared I wouldn't make it or, better yet, die at birth.

A child with a hearing impairment and pneumonia to deal with, my mother said she got me christened because she thought I wouldn't live.

But here I am, I survived the haters who bullied me in school. I guess it was to earn respect and make them feel cool.

They put up a fight with me every day, so I had to write about the bullying, torment, abuse, and all, hardly the recipe to make a person stand tall.

But I soon realised they were weak. It was attention they wanted to seek.

To make my case, thank you for the beats and bruises to my face. I often wonder why these people felt displaced because the only way they could inflict such pain was because they had so much pain.

So, about the experience of what I went through, please never let this stuff happen to you.

All alone, feeling like you are insignificant, well, you know, I turned out to be significant.

Albion School is where I was educated, although all of my years, I was hated. I don't think I had one friend to even converse with. I was beaten up religiously, almost like an activity.

In front of my sibling, the headmaster said I smell of wee. Back then, the legal system could not enforce the legality to support me.

When you have nothing, you get what you're given; I guess the subconscious mind is what makes you driven.

You don't repeat the experience once was, you wake the hell up and work hard just because.

Back to the story of when I was young and I didn't have a thing, I'd get nervous and anxious when I heard the bell ring. It was that man called J, my mother's boyfriend, the alcoholic, standing at the door, appearing catatonic.

In a drunken state, he would become irate. He would front with a knife; I would fear for my life.

It would happen in many forms, physical and violent towards all; the family was stressed to move an inch at all.

Until one day, P came along, another boyfriend singing a good song. He threw J out, and it seemed all dandy, until the criminal element started, which came in handy.

With new clothes for school and food on the table, the criminal life made the family kinda stable.

No longer searching for money or feeling to vent, this guy had it all in hand; it was money well spent.

Until Reigate, where he got caught, if he'd made it with the money from the armed robbery, he could have bought us a good life but he went to jail. We were back to the reality of life, and he set sail.

Until T came along; some would say he was a psychological abuser; I guess you could say he was also a user.

The circle of deprivation and the choices we make can lock us into a situation that we cannot fake. Although we want the best for us to succeed, we make bad choices, which make us bleed.

So, for those of you who feel like you're in a pit, time will tell if you don't want to be in it. The decisions that you make from the experience foretold, change your direction and you will want to hold, onto your experiences and the choices that you make. You will want to take all the opportunities to get that break.

So, if you can relate to me and the truth I have told, don't waste time changing your life before you're too old.

With my experiences, it's important to elaborate, but the only downfall is that it generates hate, not to the masses, but directly in my mind. I tried to find a reason for those who were unkind.

From inside of me, I think and debate. The more I think, the more it makes me hate. I try to channel the hate into good and do good things, like I know I should.

I control my anger with forgiveness, day to day, but I wake up so proud of myself every day.

Epilogue

The deep emotions, stories, and memories I have held close for so long are now documented in this book, creating a narrative of sadness, triumph, and success. My journey within these pages, in reality, has been nothing short of extraordinary.

Thoughts that I've never shared with another soul appear on the page. The challenge was to capture the events, both good and bad, as well as my feelings about them.

I had spent almost two years immersed in my memories. It had been a difficult but rewarding process, and I had put my heart and soul into it. I had faced challenging times, but I had found a way through them and emerged stronger and wiser. Now, my story has been written down on the pages of this book.

I spent my childhood engulfed in turmoil, as a dysfunctional home life full of violence, alcoholism, and bullying was my daily reality. The repercussions of these experiences followed me throughout my development, attempting to drag me into darkness.

But I refused to let what I'd endured define who I was. Despite the turmoil surrounding me, I held on tightly to the belief that a better future lay ahead for me.

Writing my story was a way of restoring my voice and finding peace. Every phrase became an acknowledgement of my strength, showing that I could overcome the hardships I'd faced.

The words spilt out from me, carrying both the burden of my history and the optimism for a better future. I grasp the finished book with a sense of fulfilment. It's not just the end of a literary quest but a personal victory.

Within its pages are my experience, my victories, and the wisdom that I've acquired along the way. By sharing my tale, I not only find myself healed, but I offer hope to those on similar journeys.

I can't help but feel a sense of serene bliss inside me. The old injuries now lay bare as badges of courage, reminding me of all I have overcome. Where once dark shadows loomed over my life, they no longer possess influence over what is happening right now. Instead, they exist as a testament to how far I have journeyed.

I take with me, on my next life adventure, a strong sense of appreciation and knowledge. My travels have demonstrated the strength found in determination, the value of self-confidence, and the potential to use stories to create change. With optimism and an unyielding soul, I move forward, ready to accept the future with open arms.

My book is a symbol of strength and an encouragement to those looking for opportunities beyond their current situation. It's my gift to the world, a homage to inspiring and enabling others.

As more and more people read it, I can be assured that my words will cause an impact; they have the potential to spark change and kindle faith in our future.

I am the architect of my own journey, and I look forward to finding joy, purpose, and meaning in every step I take towards making a difference.

My deepest thanks go out to the readers who took the time to explore my life's story. Your interest and involvement mean more than I can show you in words. Thank you for taking this journey with me and offering your reactions, focus, and sympathy.

You have not only honoured my tale but also helped to demonstrate the power of sharing it with one another. Together, I like to think that we've built a bridge of understanding and connection that surmounts any boundaries in space or time. Thank you again for being a significant part of this chapter in my life.

I would like to express my deepest gratitude to all those who have contributed to the creation and completion of this book. Without their support, guidance, and inspiration, this endeavour would not have been possible.

First and foremost, I would like to thank my family for their unwavering love and encouragement throughout this journey. Your belief in me has been the driving force behind my endeavours, and I am eternally grateful.

I extend my heartfelt appreciation to my friends and colleagues who provided valuable insights, feedback, and encouragement. Your enthusiasm and support have been invaluable, and I am fortunate to have you by my side.

A special thanks goes to the team at Austin Macauley Publishing for their expertise, professionalism, and dedication in bringing this book to life. Your tireless efforts and commitment to excellence are deeply appreciated.

I wish to express my appreciation to the reviewers and editors who meticulously reviewed and provided valuable feedback on the manuscript. Your keen eye for detail and constructive criticism have undoubtedly enhanced the quality of this work.

Lastly, I want to thank the readers who will embark on this literary journey. It is for you that this book has been written, and I hope it brings you knowledge, joy, and inspiration.

In conclusion, I extend my heartfelt appreciation to each and every individual who has played a role in the creation of this book. Your support, encouragement, and contributions have shaped it into what it is today. Thank you for being a part of this incredible journey.

Afterword

I am overwhelmed with a profound sense of gratitude and accomplishment. Writing this book whilst navigating the challenges within my own family has been a transformative journey, one that has allowed me to reflect on my life in ways I never imagined.

When I embarked on this literary endeavour, I knew I wanted to share my experiences, both the triumphs and the hardships, with the hope of inspiring others facing similar circumstances.

Living in a family with struggles can be tough. It can cast a shadow on our dreams and make us doubt our potential. But through the process of writing this book, I have come to realise that our circumstances do not define us; rather, it is our response to those circumstances that shape our character and pave the path to fulfilment.

In delving deep into my own story, I have unearthed memories and emotions that have long been buried. I have revisited moments of despair and witnessed the indomitable spirit that allowed me and my loved ones to persevere.

It hasn't been an easy road, but it has been a worthwhile one. Writing this book has not only offered me catharsis but also given me a fresh perspective on life. It has reminded me of the strength and resilience that resides within all of us, waiting to be awakened. It has taught me the power of vulnerability, for it is through sharing our struggles that we can connect and uplift one another.

Moreover, this journey has been an enlightening one. I have discovered that by embracing our own stories, we can help others find meaning in theirs. Each page I wrote was an opportunity to extend a hand to those who feel trapped in their circumstances, reminding them that they are not alone.

It is my sincerest hope that this book serves as a guiding light, igniting the fire within others to pursue their dreams and overcome obstacles, no matter how daunting they may seem.

I want to express my deepest gratitude to those who have supported me throughout this process; the unwavering love of my family, the encouragement of my friends, and the understanding of my readers.

Your belief in me and this book has been a constant source of inspiration, propelling me forward when doubts threatened to consume me.

In closing, let me emphasise that this book is not just my story; it is a testament to the strength we all have inside us. It is a reminder that even amidst the darkest of times, there is always a flicker of hope waiting to be nurtured.

May it serve as a reminder to all who read it that they possess the strength and determination to create a life filled with purpose and fulfilment, regardless of the challenges they face.

With heartfelt gratitude.

Printed in Great Britain
by Amazon